bonsai
master class

For Svetlana,

who shows me that life

should be like a bonsai:

good food, good air,

good water, good care

and lots of love.

bonsai

master class

craig coussins

Sterling Publishing Co., Inc.
New York

Library of Congress Cataloging-in-Publication Data Available

10 9 8 7 6 5 4 3 2 1

Published in 2006 by Sterling Publishing Co.., Inc.
387 Park Avenue South, New York, NY 10016

Distributed in Canada by Sterling Publishing
c/o Canadian Manda Group, 165 Dufferin Street
Toronto, Ontario, Canada M6K 3H6

For information about custom editions, special sales, premium and
corporate purchases, please contact Sterling Special Sales
Department at 800-805-5489 or specialsales@sterlingpub.com.

Printed in Thailand

Sterling ISBN-13: 978-1-4027-3547-9
ISBN-10: 1-4027-3547-2

Contents

Foreword   6

1. Understanding the basics   11

2. Evolving into a bonsai   47

3. Bonsai styles and collections   85

4. Design workshops   115

5. Asian bonsai and penjing   205

6. Bonsai and penjing display   219

7. Rocks and miniature landscapes   229

8. Associated arts   242

Index   252

Credits   255

Foreword

Walt Disney once said, "There is more treasure in books than in all the pirate's loot on Treasure Island." When we take the time to learn from books, we garner the knowledge of people who have struggled to find out their own truths. I have brought together from around the globe some great minds in the fields of bonsai, penjing, suiseki, and gongshi so that you can have access to the results of their tremendous dedication to these arts. This is not just another bonsai book: it is designed to take you on a journey toward discovering your potential as an artist by sharing that knowledge with you. Like treasure, it will not be easy to find where it is buried, but once you know how to read the map, everything will fall into place. Walt was right.

Craig Coussins, Scotland

**Grand Tetons, Wyoming —
a mysterious place full
of amazing
natural bonsai.**

About this book

Chapter 1: understanding the basics

This book will transform the reader from a grower into an artist. It's always wise to start at the beginning of any plan by going back to basics and covering the core elements of a subject. The initial sections of the book will act as a refresher course. Although it is a more advanced book on bonsai, beginners will still be able to follow the techniques to discover how to grow better bonsai and penjing, how to buy a bonsai, the horticultural requirements for different climates, how to water, feed, prune, wire and repot, seasonal care requirements and how to grow bonsai indoors.

A Japanese yew (*Taxus cuspidate*) created by Kunio Kobayashi, winner of the President's Award at the Japanese bonsai exhibition Sakufu 10.

Chapter 2: evolving into a bonsai

This chapter examines the art of bonsai and shows you how to create a bonsai. It also tells you how to look after the bonsai that you have created. Although the most important element in the creation of a bonsai is the aftercare and development, we look first at how different artists approach the initial styling of a bonsai. Observing trees in their natural surroundings is one way of gaining inspiration.

A small black pine before shaping.

A small black pine after shaping.

Chapter 3: bonsai styles and collections

There are many styles of bonsai, and this section looks at some of them — from trees in their natural landscape to outstanding examples of bonsai and penjing from growers around the world. They demonstrate how bonsai and penjing are created in different climates and environments. I have included rare images of one of the oldest trees in existence, the recently discovered Wollemi pine.

Part of the superb collection owned by New Zealand bonsai master Robert Langholm.

Chapter 4: design workshops

To create a bonsai image, an artist must understand the various design techniques. This chapter contains step-by-step demonstrations of the creation of some of these styles. I have gathered bonsai and penjing masters from Australia, Europe, America, New Zealand, Africa, Canada and Singapore to show you some of their own techniques, thus helping you to become a great bonsai artist.

The techniques include: understanding the image, suitable material, developing the image, wiring, bud development, the association between roots and branches, creating a foliage pad, creating the apex, repotting difficult trees, transplanting yamadori (collected trees), repotting large trees, finding the right pot, inverted taper correction, carving — creating age effects, such as jin, shari and uro (holes formed in trunks) — working with tropical species and unusual species for bonsai and penjing, as well as many other techniques for indoor and outdoor bonsai. Also discussed are warmer-climate species, such as *Portacularia* and *Schefflera*.

Unique images, never seen before, show John Yoshio Naka, one of the greatest bonsai teachers of the 20th century, creating a forest in 1984.

Wisteria by Kunio Kobayashi. Sensei Kobayashi is one of the leading designers and teachers of bonsai in Japan.

Chapter 5: Asian bonsai and penjing

Some of the most exciting developments in growing and styling bonsai have come out of the little country of Singapore. The quality of their bonsai and penjing is exceptional, and this is a unique look at some inspirational trees and rock arrangements.

Penjing master Lim Keow Wah takes us around the amazing penjing and gardens of Singapore. Master Lim is shown here with part of his exquisite collection.

Chapter 6: bonsai and penjing display

Displaying bonsai, both in exhibition and in your collection at home, is in itself an art. Paul Goff and I look at the tokonoma, or display alcoves, in detail.

Alcove display is an integral part of most Japanese homes. This tokonoma image is from Daichi Bonsai in the UK, and was created by Alexander Kennedy, who runs one of the outlets.

Chapter 7: rocks and miniature landscapes

This chapter looks at art forms that are often exhibited with bonsai and penjing: rockscapes, with and without plants, and landscapes in miniature. I have included pictures of some of the wonderful natural rockscapes that inspire us to recreate them in miniature.

Located in northwest Wyoming, the Grand Teton National Park protects stunning mountain scenery. This is the kind of image that we like to recreate when making landscape plantings.

Chapter 8: associated arts

There are many associated arts that work well alongside bonsai. Suiseki, sansui-seki and toyamakei are some of the Japanese names for the different shapes of viewing stones.

Chinese scholar's stones, gongshi, are fast becoming popular among both bonsai growers and those interested in Oriental art. Drawing on images from nature and various stone collections, I have shown some of the many different styles that are available. These are displayed on their own stands, daiza, and in suibans, trays.

Kemin Hu, America's leading authority on Chinese scholar's stones, gongshi, explains the stones.

Internationally acclaimed daiza carver Sean Smith writes a section on carving daiza and displaying suiseki. Images from a Singapore exhibition show the different styles of stones.

The scholar's home — a display of Chinese scholar's stones from the He Shi Chuang Collection, Suzhou, China.

盆栽

chapter 1
understanding the basics

Bonsai has become one of the most popular hobbies worldwide. Some hobbies, such as ikebana, are based on artistic expression, while growing cacti is based on horticultural knowledge for that particular range of species. Bonsai straddles the artistic and horticultural worlds.

Understanding the basics

Yes, we need to know how to take care of, grow and maintain the tree, but, left to its own devices, the tree will grow in a random style and will take many years to achieve its mature image. Artistic input means that we can develop that tree into a miniature image of its final shape in a very short period. Keeping the roots and branches dense and healthy, while growing the plant in a shallow container, and pruning and shaping the branches into a tree-like structure, will eventually give the illusion of a mature, full-grown or very old tree.

Growing bonsai is an art form. Reading this book will contribute to your artistic knowledge, as will going to classes held by bonsai masters. Without the artistic knowledge, it can be difficult to understand the techniques that are required to get the tree to this point of its development into a bonsai. Perspective, placement and design are all part of this process. Looking at nature and taking ideas from the forests, plains, deserts and mountains can help us to become better bonsai artists.

Understanding perspective is probably the most important element in bonsai design. We are creating an illusion of something that, in reality, can be anything from fifty to many hundred percent larger. Skill is necessary to do this, and some of the projects in this book look at different ways of creating such an illusion. For example, with perspective-planting, the illusion of distance is achieved by planting a tall bonsai slightly toward the front of the pot while placing a similar-shaped, but much smaller, tree slightly to the rear and to one side of the pot. Later chapters showcase the work of bonsai masters from around the globe who explain their thoughts and designs. This should give you some insight into how different artists approach a subject.

In many countries, other than in the West and Japan, bonsai are called by other names. In Vietnam, the style of planting preferred to bonsai is called hon non bo, and in China, it is called penjing. Of course, the art has developed in different ways around the world, and no more so than in the West. The generic name of bonsai was taken originally from the Chinese pentsai nearly one thousand years ago, and was translated by the Japanese as bonsai. Today, the art of bonsai practiced in places outside Japan can be quite different to that practiced inside the country.

Naturally, each country has its own species and climatic conditions. Also, the practitioners of the art of bonsai are at many differing levels of competence. As a teacher of bonsai, I feel that it is always better to start my books with a "back to basics" section. In this way, newer growers, as well as those who are more experienced, have the opportunity to discover new techniques or come up with suggestions that will help them to develop their abilities.

What is a bonsai?

Around the world, bonsai has different meanings. In China, where potted trees can be a few inches or 50 feet (15 m) tall, the art of bonsai, or punjing (penjing), as it is known, has no real limits on size. I have wandered through a garden of ancient, potted trees that had massive, thick trunks 3 feet (1 m) across, while being 5 feet (1.5 m) tall.

What determines whether a plant in a pot is a bonsai is if it looks like a tree rather than a shrub stuck in a nice ceramic container and passed off as a bonsai.

In purely technical terms, a bonsai is a tree that has had its roots and foliage pruned in a certain way so that it generates multiple growth points along the root or branch. Reducing the distances between these internodes makes the tree stronger, and thus able to live in an environment where it is supported by these dense roots and ramified (with a dense twig structure) branches. In other words, you reduce the tree by creating a miniature version of a full-sized tree. When a bonsai or penjing is mature, it looks exactly like a full-sized tree.

The illusion is in the size. A small, five-year-old bonsai tree can look like a tree that is fifty years old and 82 feet (25 m) tall. The difference is not just the height, but what you do to provide a successful growing environment that will allow that tree to survive in good health. This is the technique of ensuring the subsequent development of fine feeder roots and fine twigs on the branches of the bonsai.

Bonsai are divided into tiny, small, medium- and large-sized trees. Very large trees are sometimes called yard bonsai as they are too large to be classed as bonsai. This is subjective, but also practical. See page 89 for a more detailed discussion of size.

While not covering every type of tree used for bonsai, I have photographed some interesting species that may inspire you to re-create their shapes. These include kauri, pohutukawa, pine (*Pinus*), *Ficus*, banksia, juniper and oak.

A Singapore garden of large, potted, ancient trees.

Watering — the basic requirement for survival

Water filtration and timer setup.

We really need to understand watering as a tool for growing bonsai and penjing. Overwatering and underwatering can damage growth in a cool or temperate climate. Both are less of a problem in tropical climates, but even then, correct watering is important.

It is vital to water your trees correctly, as the following story illustrates. A woman bought a very nice, mature, outdoor, elm bonsai from a grower. She paid a lot for it, and was given a list of care instructions. She asked if she could take the bonsai home first to see if it would fit in with her garden design. As she was known to the grower, he allowed her to do this. She returned the tree the following week with the comment: "Look, the bonsai that you were going to sell me is dead." Looking at the shrivelled mass of brown leaves on a bonsai that had taken him nearly twenty years to develop, the grower was understandably upset. He asked the woman for a blow-by-blow account of what she had done since taking the tree away a few days ago. She said that the tree looked so pretty, with its bright, shiny leaves, that she decided that it would look really good inside the house. She placed the tree in a bright, very sunny, window and then went to visit a friend for the weekend. When she returned three days later, the tree was in this state. "So," she said, "this bonsai must have been dying when I took it away." The grower asked her what she had done about watering the bonsai while she was away. "Watering? What do you mean, watering? I didn't know that a bonsai needed to be watered." The grower asked her whether she

Thin tubes from a main hose, with dripfeed nipples.

had read the care instructions. "I am far too busy to read all that stuff. I wanted a bonsai that you could just admire, not water or do other jobs like that." She had managed to fry the poor tree. However, it was not dead, and, after chopping back half of the shrivelled branches, sealing the cuts and removing the dried leaves, the grower watered the tree well, placed the whole sorry mess in a large, clear, plastic sack and treated it like a giant cutting. After a couple of weeks, new buds started popping out around the trunk. However, it would be another three years before the bonsai regained some of its former glory.

So, to conclude, yes, watering is important. And we cannot assume that even the most intelligent person necessarily understands the requirements for a bonsai's basic needs.

Watering — essential information

Incorrect watering is one of the biggest killers of bonsai. The tips below are drawn from thirty years' experience of watering bonsai.

- Either too little or too much water may cause the roots to dry out or to rot.
- A free-draining soil will assist in the transition of water through the pot. Compacted soil is easy to spot as water will collect on the surface. Ideally, when you water bonsai, the water should flow freely through the soil.
- Keep the soil moist in the summer, but water less in winter. In winter, just keep the soil damp and do not let it dry out. A bonsai is not a cactus: it needs a damp soil to keep the roots alive through its dormant period.
- In most cool-to-temperate climates, watering once a day during the growing period is usually enough, but check your soil. In hotter months, watering will need to be done up to three times a day. In a hot country, leave the trees in some shade for part of the day to keep them cooler. In some countries, hot winds can damage the tree by drying it out very quickly.
- If your soil's surface is looking a bit light in color, it is probably dry. However, check just under the surface.

On larger trees, you may need up to four feeder nipples.

Your bonsai will appreciate being sprayed or misted once a day in the spring and autumn months, and up to twice a day in the summer period. If you have a hothouse, greenhouse or glasshouse and store your trees there in the winter, a weekly spray is acceptable. However, you will need to make sure that the structure of the glasshouse allows adequate ventilation. Paint on the liquid shade cover used for glasshouses. You do not want to give much heat to temperate-climate species.

- In winter storage, outdoor bonsai require a weekly check, but if the soil is damp, leave it alone as the tree will not take up more water.
- Indoor bonsai require watering once a day in warmer months, but every two or three days in winter and spring. If you have central heating or an air conditioner running, the soil will dry out faster. Keep the soil slightly damp, but not soggy.
- Succulents need little water for the three months of colder weather in temperate or colder climates, so bear that in mind if you keep *Portulacaria*, *Crassula* or money- or jade-tree bonsai (see page 194, Jim Smith). They are succulents and need to be watered once a month in winter. Larger specimens may need more frequent watering. If you are in a warm climate, water once a week. It is best to speak to your local specialist if you are unsure.
- Spring, in colder climes, means that you need to start regular watering again. But it is only necessary if the bonsai requires it. In colder climates, during the winter period, outdoor bonsai need little, if any, water — if they are kept outside, of course. In any case, protect them from winds and frosts if possible.

In addition to dripfeed nipples, you may need extra water basins to create humidity in very dry climates.

(Images taken at the Cordoba Bonsai Club, Spain.)

How to water your bonsai

Automatic watering systems are very popular and reasonably easy to set up. Use a sequenced automatic time switch. Although it is sometimes called a "computer watering system," it is really just a simple timer that starts and shuts off water in a desired sequence. This is useful when you want to water some of the trees at a certain time, or more than once a day in hot weather. You can rig up the hoses to a gadget, sometimes called an octopus, that has around six to eight hose-attachment nipples. They can be set to go off in a sequence that allows a different hose to water a different section each time the timer starts. The timer can be set to go on and off six times throughout the day. If one section needs watering twice, attach a Y-piece to two shorter hoses on different sides of the octopus. Here is what I set up in my own place.

- One and six water the deciduous trees for ten minutes each. The timer is set to 7:00 a.m. and 5:00 p.m.
- Two comes on after one and waters the pines and conifers for six minutes in hot weather. It is set for 4:00 p.m.
- Three waters the *Ficus*, willows and other water-loving plants for twelve minutes. It is set for 4:30 p.m.
- Four waters the trees growing in beds, such as yamadori. It is set for 5:00 p.m.
- Five waters the rest of the garden plants and borders. It is set for 5:30 p.m.
- If I need to water during the day in exceptional heat, I can do so by hose without touching the computer because the water faucet is rigged with a split tap to allow a separate hose connector.

Watering systems: a multiple-hose outlet for different areas.

The kit comprises a water computer timer, a multiple-hose distributor unit for six hoses and a water reducer that changes the flow from the hose into the narrower hose for the drip-feeder nipples. I also use different nipples that allow different rates of water — 2–20 pints an hour — to travel through the feeder nipples.

There are some drawbacks to auto systems. The drip feeds can clog or stop working, battery-powered systems are less reliable than mains-powered systems and, after softening in the sun on a warm day, junctions in the piping may suddenly come apart when pressured up. Auto systems also continue to water during rainy spells when the tree does not need more water. Some systems have a "cloudy day" feature, but it can be very warm on a cloudy day, and the soil may still need water. You are therefore stuck between a rock and a hard place. If you

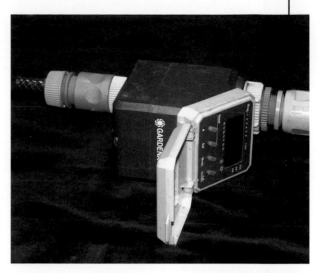

Watering systems: timer computer.

turn that feature off, the tree will be watered, whether it needs it or not. Now, that is not too bad in a hot climate, as the temperature is more than likely to be constant and rain will be rare in the warmer seasons. In humid climates, the system is, of course, not so good. In any case, the soil should be free-draining and the water should run through fast. Use wooden wedges to tilt bonsai, such as conifers, that need less water and will benefit from free runoff. Ensure that the pot and wedge are secure and unlikely to topple off the bench. Alternatively, remove the drips from the pots every other day.

There are more expensive systems with a sensor that determines moisture levels in the soil. However, even these are not completely satisfactory because one tree's water needs may be radically different from another's.

Despite these drawbacks, automatic watering systems are not a great problem and can be a benefit if you are off on vacation. Just ask your neighbor to check that all of the pots are being watered and that the soil is damp. Point out the potential weaknesses in the system, and a good neighbor should be able to manage it successfully.

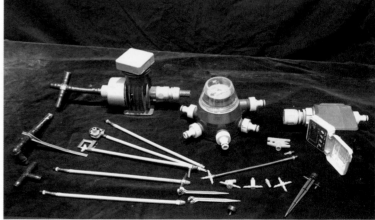

Watering systems: various heads and sections for an automatic system.

Using a hose

I still need to use a hose in other locations and I always attach an adjustable trigger spray or multispray unit to it. Water pressure is crucial. If you have a lot of trees, you will need a powerful spray that is still fine enough not to wash out the soil or damage the buds.

Hose spraying is most growers' normal method of watering as this can be a more controlled way of making sure that the right trees get what they need. Use the adjustable trigger spray to control the intensity of water delivery. Feeder units, supplied by most of the major plant-food companies, can easily be added. Just make sure that you do not overfeed.

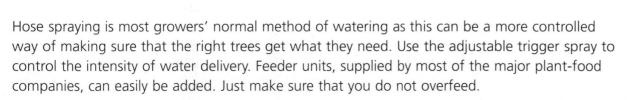

bonsai master class

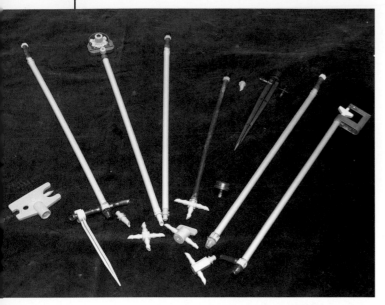

Watering systems: various heads.

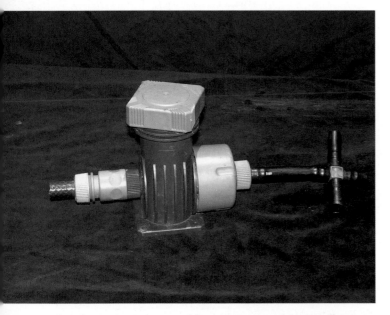

**A hose pressure-reducer to allow
drip-watering to function.**

Winter and summer watering

Winter and summer watering depends on the climatic
requirements. Essentially, you may water anywhere from once to
three times in any one day. I would suggest that it may be better
to water twice on a hot day and mist once or twice, damping
down the benching and ground to create some humidity around
the bonsai or penjing. This is not essential in cooler months.
However, it is essential for species with fine needles, like
Sequoiadendron giganteum (giant sequoia), which normally
grows at 5,000 feet (1,524 m) in its natural habitat in the
Yosemite region of California, where the air is generally moist.

Misting the foliage

Misting is giving the foliage a fine spray. While part of the general
watering, spraying the foliage acts like rain. If you have warm
days, the foliage may dry up through dehydration. In most cases,
misting will replenish the moisture. Extra misting can be very
important in warmer climates, in hot weather and under shade
nets. *Pinus* (pine) needs more misting than deciduous
Cryptomeria. Sequoia needs daily misting, while other species
need misting every two or three days. Misting cleans the leaves,
reduces pests and, as Chase Rosade, the famous master, once
said, highlights the small webs of spider mite.

Deciduous trees can trap water between their leaves, and it is
therefore best to spray them once a week, or three times in hot
weather. Water droplets will not act as magnifying glasses and
burn the leaves. That is a myth. In colder climates, misting is
rarely done in winter. In these cooler climates, the soil is kept
barely damp through the winter months. Many deciduous trees
need very little light and water when under winter storage,
although there is the danger of forgetting all about them. Just
remind yourself to check them at least once a week. I will
reiterate that while misting is not the only watering given, it
forms part of the general overall watering program. Indoor bonsai
need humidity levels kept up, and if you grow tropical trees, you
will need to mist two or three times a day.

Subtropical climate

The subtropical climate is generally warm and humid, but some
cold days can occur. The rainy season is more prevalent and the
summers can be extremely hot.

Tropical — mountains and lowlands

The tropical climate does not experience cooler weather except in the mountains. I find that bonsai and penjing growers are noticing changes in recent weather conditions that can be partially attributed to what is happening in warmer climates. I teach bonsai in many countries, and I live in Scotland. We have seen a marked change in temperatures, humidity levels and rainfall over the most recent years. I am an avid photographer of landscapes and have been fortunate to travel to many countries, both as a bonsai teacher and as a photographer. The reduction of natural habitat is, in my opinion, a very serious issue, and we should be aware of the changes caused by deforestation around the world.

Deforestation is causing climate changes, as are other factors. This means that temperate and cooler areas are having warmer, and sometimes wetter, weather than they had in previous years. Many very hot countries have high mountains. Nepal, for example, has a vast area of mountainous terrain, as well as jungles in the lowlands. In Africa, where the plains can be very dry in the summer months, Tanzania's Mount Kilimanjaro — celebrated by Ernest Hemingway in *The Snows of the Kilimanjaro* — is, due to its altitude, permanently covered in snow. Its ice cap will probably disappear by 2020 due to the deforestation of the lower slopes for pasture, which causes a change in the microclimate of the mountain. That indicator shows that other mountains with glacial ice caps across the globe will lose their ice if similar deforestation to create grazing areas at the mountain's base occurs. Using this analogy, I remember my own bonsai teacher talking about microclimates nearly thirty years ago. He taught us that each area, each bench and each pot can have its own microclimate. What you do to that tree can affect the tree's microclimate. Understand the tree's microclimate, and you will understand what it is telling you. Short of talking to the trees, learning everything possible about what affects us in terms of climate and conditions is the only way to understand what the bonsai are saying.

Apparently, worldwide deforestation could create higher temperatures in some parts of the world, causing loss of ice caps, rising waters, and, in some cases, more rain. We can do very little about these changes, but we should be aware that they may affect us in the short term. Recently, in some countries, we have seen exceptional storms, high winds, freezing winters, excessive rain, and unusual weather patterns. Farmers in some temperate countries have lost crops through excessive rainfall. Anything that I suggest about caring for your trees should therefore be read with the understanding that the weather is beyond my control.

Misting systems in a larger collection.

Mike Sullivan, of the UK, makes sure that his mister is at hand when designing.

Looking at trees in nature for inspiration

The ancient horse chestnut (*Aesculus hippocastanum*) originates in Albania, Turkey and Greece. Here, it is in an English landscape, where it has been grown as an ornamental tree for centuries.

A cottonwood on the Red Plateau in the Hurricane Sands Desert of Utah, near St. George. My brother lives down the road in Las Vegas, so I am often here. I use an all-terrain vehicle (ATV) when exploring these desert plateaus, and find some amazing tree images, as well as fantastic rockscapes.

Mountain mahogany (*Cercocarpus ledifolius*) on the sides of Great Basin in northern Nevada. This drought-resistant tree is common only on dry hillsides and ridges between 6,000 to 9,000 feet (1,828–2,743 m). It is a small tree, with a tendency to be round-crowned and sprawling, often showing shari on the trunk.

English beech (*Fagus engleriana*).

A Utah juniper (*Sabina osteosperma* syn. *Juniperus osteosperma*) from the *Cupressaceae* (cypress) family. As you can see, this is a small tree that could well be great yamadori.

Scots pine (*Pinus sylvatica*). Growing like this on an island, where the natural tail-off can be quite harsh, creates an almost rectangular outline and flat top for this forest.

Aspens in the autumn. Scientists studying the trembling aspen (*Populus tremuloides*) have concluded that individual clones can survive for 10,000 years or more, making them possibly the longest-lived organisms on the planet. Aspens also spread out from the rootstock, making them the largest living organisms in the world. In Utah, there is an aspen clone, nicknamed "Pando," that could be the largest-known living organism in the world. This aspen group contains 50,000 trees, spanning 200 acres (80 ha). It is estimated to weigh 6,600 tons and has one root. From this single aspen tree root comes bark, leaves and stems with a shared genetic characteristic. I lay down under this tall group and photographed the falling leaves of "Pando."

Tiny natural bonsai. These trees are many hundreds of years old. They live on the tree line just before the high desert. The tree line, or timber line, is the edge of the habitat in which trees are capable of growing. Beyond the tree line, inappropriate environmental conditions make it impossible for trees to grow. At the tree line, tree growth is often very stunted and affected by wind. The last trees form low, dense matted bushes. These are known as krummholz, from the German for "twisted wood." Trees grow shorter the nearer they are to the inhospitable climate, until they simply stop growing. My friend John Whiteis, helped me to take this image at around 11,000 feet (3,352 m), during a 15,000-foot (4,572 m) climb.

Aspens in the snow. One of my favorite images is aspens in deep snow.

Common European juniper (*Juniperus communis*). Collecting in this environment can be a mix of good and bad. The problem is that these trees are very deep-rooted and a lot of digging is required. Treat them like giant cuttings and plant them in pure pumice to get the best root development. They do not like their roots being cut, so be very careful to take as much root as possible, and have feeder roots near the trunk. Seal all major cuts or the tree will die. The best time to collect is during early spring or mid-summer — both dormant periods.

Indoor bonsai and outdoor bonsai

Outdoor or indoor trees?

Outdoor trees are those that suit the climatic conditions of the place where you live. Indoor trees are those from warmer climates that are grown in cooler or temperate areas. For example, a *Ficus* that can grow happily in Singapore will need some protection in cooler climates, whereas most pines are best suited to cooler regions and will not do well in warmer parts of the world. (Images in this section show trees in nature for reference.)

I once had a discussion in Florida with an experienced bonsai artist on the virtues of keeping pines and other cooler-climate trees in such a warm place as Miami. Growing them indoors with air-conditioning would not work because the air-conditioning units dry the air, which would be detrimental to the trees. However, growers in warm climates can experiment by introducing humidity to an air-conditioned atmosphere. The results may be successful.

Behavior of different trees in different parts of the world

In cooler climates, deciduous trees drop their leaves in the autumn. In warmer climates, the leaves sometimes drop, depending on the species, but normally deciduous trees keep their leaves and just keep growing. In the warmer regions of China, for example, the elm (*Ulmus*) retains its leaves year round, while in the cooler parts, it drops its leaves. Such information is important to bonsai growers as it will determine how they should keep their bonsai.

Trees one, three or four?
Designs from nature's perspective in planting

I found these cottonwood trees on the Red Plateau, in the Hurricane Sands Desert, Utah, where I like to go ATV-driving. Local drivers call this group the "Three Apostles".

A single cottonwood in a desert environment provides a design image to consider recreating.

Three cottonwoods are an equally attractive design image.

In the case of four cottonwoods, as in nature, it is best to plant three and to set one to one side (we tend to call this tree "he who stands alone").

Indoor bonsai

Always remember that indoor trees in cooler climates are outdoor trees in warmer areas. Some Chinese elms (*Ulmus parvifolia*), *Serissa foetida* (tree of a thousand stars), *Sageretia theezans* (Chinese sweet plum), *Conocarpus erectus* (buttonwood), *Ehretia buxifolia* (*Carmona microphylla*), *Punica granatum* (pomegranate), *Brassaia actinophylla* (*Schefflera*), *Ficus* species, *Portulacaria* and *Crassula* live happily outdoors in warmer climates, but would not survive in colder areas, especially in the colder months of the year.

Some trees, such as Chinese elms (*Ulmus parvifolia*), can be kept inside during cooler weather and outside after spring to enjoy the warmer weather; many of the indoor bonsai sold are this species. If kept outside and acclimatized, these trees may eventually drop their leaves in the winter as they become hardy. I have many such trees, and it is interesting to note that some of the Chinese elms will retain some of their leaves in winter even if kept outside. I should point out that these leaves are sparse, while trees of the same species kept inside remain fully leafed, although the leaves are not as lush as those of spring and summer.

Old pines along one of the stony lake shores near Grand Teton, Wyoming.

Dropping leaves on "indoor trees"

I often receive inquiries from panicking growers who are worried that their little "indoor trees" are dropping their leaves. Although evergreen, elms and most other indoor species can still drop leaves, even when kept inside. It is a natural and ongoing process. The dropping leaves are usually one or two years old and are replaced by either new leaves at the end of the branch or leaves in the same area if the branch is pruned. That means that if you prune and pinch out the growth regularly, the tree will become thicker. If you do not, the tree will just grow to length and all of the branches will become long and thin.

Most indoor trees require a minimum temperature of 50°F (10°C). They will occasionally drop their leaves in response to lower light conditions, unless you can provide a suitable environment for them.

An old hawthorn (*Crataegus*) in the El Torcal Mountains, southern Spain.

Eucalyptus hang precariously on the cliffs beside the Three Sisters at Katoomba, in the Blue Mountains, near Sydney, Australia.

Old junipers cling onto rocks for centuries around Flaming Gorge, Utah.

Lighting for indoor bonsai

When growing trees completely indoors, you will need light. It should be noted that light ingress is variable at different times of the year, and growing in a window area may not always be the best way to achieve success. Let me explain why. The light coming in from a window is reduced in lumens (light factor) while increasing the heat, unless the window has been treated with ultraviolet screening. Some growers suggest that the light coming through a window can be reduced by as much as 50 percent. In the spring to summer period, the sun gradually rises in the sky and is quite high. This means that the light is in a downward direction, and so the tree will start to grow quickly toward the light source. In a very sunny window, that could also mean that the bonsai is actually being fried, instead of just getting light. There is no free-flowing air and the glass generates heat; the result is a dried-out pot. That means that you will need to cater for the regular watering, misting, and rotation of the bonsai.

As light levels reduce in the autumn to early spring period, the sun is low on the horizon and the direct light becomes less intense in the midwinter period. That means that the tree is not getting enough light to function. Some leaves will fall off and eventually the tree itself will fail. Watering can also be a problem, as bonsai are often over-watered during the darker months.

Artificial lighting will work very well for many species, so you can grow bonsai that are suitable for indoor cultivation in windowless rooms. The lighting setup is reasonably simple, but needs a little planning.

Space is crucial. Daylight tubes, which offer 95 percent daylight, are essential. A spread of light is best, rather than just one light tube. The bonsai need as much light as possible from all sides, or you may get heavy top growth and weaker side growth. The light should generally be left on for around twelve to fifteen hours each day. A timer switch will enable you to do this, provided that you make sure that the timer switch is working. The lights will function at full strength for at least one year. After that, the light will start to reduce in strength, and so should be replaced as a matter of course.

I suggest that you use a bank of three lights in a shallow curve over the trees. Put them on three timers that switch on at sequential periods to emulate the movement of the sun. The first one should be on for eight hours, the middle one should come on after four hours and the last light should come on as the first light goes out. The overhead light goes out after twelve hours, while the last light stays on for eight hours. That allows even light on both sides of the tree instead of just in one place.

The shelf should be strong enough to hold a shallow, watertight container full of fine gravel, which should be kept moist. Trees should also be rotated to get even growth. In warmer weather, they can be taken outside, as long as the temperature does not fall below 55°F (13°C).

Pines that are over 32 feet (10 m) tall look like miniatures on this rock face in Yosemite, California.

Pines meet the mighty waterfall of the Yellowstone Grand Canyon, Wyoming, with its multicolored, steep walls.

General notes: indoor bonsai and penjing

Indoor bonsai need light, but not a window that is facing the sun all day. That will fry the tree. Note when windows get light during the day and choose one that is not in sunshine all day long. Windows reduce the light by a factor of twenty, but heat can build up quickly under glass. Bonsai need a lot of light — not necessarily sunlight, but a good source of bright light. The better solution is growing under artificial lights, such as 95 percent daylight tubes.

- Placing bonsai on a shelf in the room is fine if the shelf gets a lot of light during the day.
- To ensure that your bonsai get even growth and do not just grow on one side only, it is important to turn them regularly.
- Do not put your bonsai on a windowsill where you pull the drapes at night. That will create a damp, cold place and will chill the bonsai. A good, even room temperature is the answer.
- It is not wise to place any plants on top of electrical units, such as televisions. Most generate heat. Also, water may drip into the unit.

Outdoor bonsai

This beautiful view of a juniper illustrates great perspective, and is useful as a landscape design. I took this photograph in northern Wyoming.

All trees need light. Some need bright sun and others need some shade. Most bonsai need sun. Keeping a tree in permanent shade will result in one of three things: the growth will become thin and spindly as the tree reaches out to find more light; the lack of light will reduce the tree's ability to photosynthesize and will therefore make the growth pale and weak; and, finally, lack of light will cause the tree to die back in the areas that are not receiving adequate light.

Growing bonsai suitable for outdoor cultivation releases you from a lot of pressure as you do not have to worry about the vagaries of the weather affecting their growth. When the warmer months start, you can place most indoor bonsai trees in a suitable position outside to get as much light as they require.

Placement is important, as is turning the tree. Placing a tree on a bench and not turning it at least once a week will mean that one side of the tree will grow faster and more healthily than the other. The development of any tree is dependent on the available light, so keeping one side in shade is not helping your bonsai.

Bonsai are grown in an artificial environment. Their soil levels are small and their root structure is tight. The available space for growth is less than in nature, and so the tree's placement can be good or bad, depending on your growing facility.

In cooler months, the tree will need all of the light that it can get. Cooler months in temperate climates mean lower sun and darker days, while summer sun can scorch and the tree will need some shade during the day. Watching how the sun affects the light in your garden or yard will quickly tell you the best spot and the worst spot. Moving light levels will indicate the best part of the garden or yard in which to put your bonsai.

In warmer climates, a bonsai should normally be placed so that it receives some shade at some point in the day. If not, you will need to rotate it more often. More watering will also be required in hotter climates. As long as you remember when to water, your trees should grow well.

Placement and light: position and shade

To summarize:

• outdoor bonsai need plenty of free air circulation;

• they need some sun, but also some shade if the sun is hot;

• do not place bonsai tight up against a wall or a fence as that will cause damage to the back of the tree. Do not place the tree anywhere near recently painted or creosoted fence panels because this can kill it;

• to ensure even light, and thus even growth, all the way around the bonsai, turn your trees every week. One easy tip is to place a plant marker at the front of every pot. The markers should all be facing the same way, so that when you turn the trees, you can immediately see whether any have been forgotten.

One-sided growth on bonsai

One of the most common problems with bonsai is one-sided growth, or one-sided health. Laziness is the culprit: the more bonsai you have, the less you are inclined to turn your trees on a regular basis. It is very important to turn your trees regularly. The minimum is a half-turn every week, so that over the month you get even growth. Otherwise, the tree will die on the side facing away from the light, while the side facing the light will become very untidy. (This also applies to all houseplants.)

Winter light for deciduous bonsai in cold climates is not so important, but fresh air is. In fact, all bonsai need a free flow of air around the foliage. This stops turgid air conditions and reduces the possibility of fungal infections on the leaves, roots and soil. Mildew, or botrytis, is the most common of these, and usually appears in damp, cool conditions. You can treat it with a copper fungicide, but with correct care, it should not happen in the first place. Copper fungicide must not penetrate the soil at any stage as that may damage the mycelium, or beneficial fungi, in the tree's root system.

It is important to ensure that you get good light, or as much light as possible, in the growing seasons. Trees in pots rarely appreciate full sun as the sun quickly dries out the shallow soil. The leaves, getting no respite from the heat, will shrivel. It is wiser to provide some shade for part of the day. That is fairly easy to arrange if you watch your garden on a sunny day to check how the sun hits it.

Remember that it's not a good idea to place bonsai against a wall or fence unless the foliage is well away from the surface. It is extremely important in all cases to rotate the trees for even light.

Hanging over a rocky escarpment, this Ponderosa pine, in Zion Canyon, Utah, displays a perfect cascade.

The mechanics of bonsai

Soil

Almost all soils contain four basic components: mineral particles, water, air and organic matter. The fertility of soil is directly influenced by the pH through the solubility of nutrients. A pH lower than 5.5 will mean that many nutrients become very soluble and are readily leached from the soil structure. At higher pH levels, the nutrients become insoluble and plants cannot easily extract them. The best take-up for nutrients is a pH value of around 6.0 to 7.2.

All bonsai soils need to be free draining. This means that the soil does not hold too much water, collect water on the surface or remain soaked for long after watering. Air needs to get through the soil medium. Most commercial bonsai soils are created to drain rapidly.

Some of these soils are sterile and require added nutrients. They are not mixed with components, such as organic material, but are sold on their own merits. Most of these dry soils need to be sieved to extract the dust or the soil will compact and cause problems within a short period.

Many prebagged Japanese bonsai soils are now used around the globe, sold under different brand names. Many are also known by their generic names. They include such soils as Akadama (general), Kiryu/Kiryuzuna (conifers) and Kanuma (azaleas and acid-lovers). All three basic Japanese soils are sterile mixes and not fertile. This means that you will need to add fertilizer to ensure that the tree receives the correct nutrients. A Japanese soil called Fujiu/Fujizuna is a volcanic granular material that comes from Mount Fuji and is similar to pumice. It is very good for rooting some collected material, such as juniper. Another soil relatively recent to horticulture outside Japan is Keto/Ketotsuki. This is an organic, fertile mix like sticky clay or peat muck (a mix of peat and clay that is used to retain soil edges on slab plantings). Keto is also used for making rock plantings, holding the plant in place due to its adhering abilities. I make small balls of this material and put them under the tree when planting on rock. The claylike material holds the tree in place. When the roots have settled, they will grow through the material. You can also use peat muck for this job. Your local bonsai specialist will help you to choose the most suitable soil.

Clay in bonsai soils

Many growers throw their hands up when talking about clay because it has a reputation for drying out and not being able to reinstate itself. The clay content of any soil shows a significant and positive relation to the soil moisture constants. The effect of clay water retention is higher than that of the other soil properties, indicating that clay content is the most effective soil property influencing water retention in soil moisture constants. Clay is a commonly used soil additive in China and many other countries. The downside for growers of bonsai and penjing is that the clay needs to be kept moist. However, why would you allow your soil to dry out to that point? As long as you water your trees, clay additive should not be an issue. If the clay dries out, it is relatively certain that the bonsai or penjing will also have dried out. If the tree has passed the wilting point, it will be dying or dead already.

A basic knowledge of the soil-to-water relationship is essential for knowing what kind of bonsai can or cannot be grown in a soil that has clay content.

Soil water retention is a basic soil property that influences available water, drainage, water stress on plants and the passage of water through the soil levels in a bonsai pot. The bonsai will develop best when the soil-to-water retention is kept at the level where the tree does not start to wilt or dry out. That is known as the PWP, or permanent wilting point. This is determined by the percentage of water remaining in the soil after watering and the subsequent drainage through the soil — between a few hours and up to two days. Initially, volcanic clays, such as Akadama, are in a dry state and the structure of the clay allows water both to pass through and be retained for a short period.

The breakdown of these "soils", while important, is not generally of interest to most growers. However, it is worth knowing something about the three most common pre-bagged soils.

Akadama

Akadama is a volcanic, semi- to hard-clay soil that comes in a number of forms. The generic name is also branded, but can come from different sources. It is sold in one-, two- or three-line qualities. These lines are in red and are shown on the bags. They indicate the hardness or softness of the clay. Three-line Akadama is the hardest. It is not always good for potting as the harder granules do not break down as easily as the two line's. As the feeder roots develop on such species as maple (*Acer*), softer soil is better for the vigor of the tree. The harder form is better for holly (*Ilex crenata*), and I have also used it successfully on hawthorn (*Crataegus*) and firethorn (*Pyracantha*).

Akadama is excellent for developing finer feeder roots. Once the tree is established, add some inorganic material, such as Kiryu, washed grit or river sand, with a minimum size of 2 to 4mm. I have used Akadama for over twenty-five years to strike cuttings and root yamadori from pines (*Pinus*) to *Lonicera*. It can be mixed with peat and used to make air-layers, and is great when used with Rooterpot.

Akadama on its own is a general soil for many bonsai species. Although growers have used it unmixed for years, they now find that mixing Akadama with other mediums, such as peat, or other specialist soils, is better for the health of many bonsai, such as *Ficus*, fruiting trees and *Sequoia*. I find that beech (*Fagus*), with its shallow rooting system, thrives in an organic and Akadama mix. Getting the right soil mix will depend on your climatic requirements, as well as the kind of soil in the place where you live. Akadama has a nominal pH of 6.8. Always sift the fines out and do not use them anywhere near your bonsai, especially as a top dressing, as they will wash in and compact the soil.

Tieu Canh: a Vietnamese landscape in miniature.

Vietnamese Tieu Canh.

This beach scene is in North Island, New Zealand. The miniature Vietnamese scenes, Tieu Canh, have many similarities.

Kanuma

Kanuma is similar to Akadama, but is used for acid-loving plants, such as azaleas, satsukis, ericas and stewartias. It is normally a yellow granule with a high water-absorption rate, and is excellent for rooting azalea and rhododendron cuttings. Kanuma can be mixed with peat to increase its ability to retain some nutrients. Generally, this is at a 20 percent peat to 80 percent Kanuma ratio, but check the local best practices.

Kanuma has a pH of 4.5 to 5.

Kiryu

Kiryu is excellent for conifers, and is used neat from the bag. But that said, it is pretty sterile and I prefer to make a mix of Akadama and Kiryu to ensure good root development. For most pines, I use a 50–50 mix, but as they develop, I increase the Kiryu part of the soil to 70, 80 or even 90 percent. I tend not to use organic with Kiryu as it can cause the soil to become solid. Free-draining soil is the core principle of all bonsai soils, and none of them will compact if prepared correctly. Sieving is important to remove fine dust because that does compact the soil. It is good to use the larger granules of these imported soils at the bottom of the pot, and then to graduate to a smaller size at the surface. In fact, the bags of most brands recommend this practice. Most bonsai nurseries sell sets of sieves to help you to get the grading right.

Research is being undertaken to discover methods of reducing the nitrogen leaching into the environment, mostly for conservation of our biodiversity. The most promising research involves the use of high-fired clay materials (similar to some types of cat litter) that absorb phosphorus and ammonium. Zeolite is currently used for this purpose, and Kiryu is a zeolite.

The pH of Kiryu is around 6.8. You should use acid-based fertilizers on acid-loving plants.

What is the pH of your soils?

The pH is an indication of whether or not the soil is acid, neutral or alkaline. The soil reaction and condition is measured in pH units. When growing bonsai, you will need to be aware of this. What soil mix is acid and what is neutral? Both are important for the health of the bonsai. The pH also tells you what food is correct for the bonsai. Azaleas are acid-loving, while maples are not. Some conifers prefer a slightly acid soil, while others like a slightly alkaline soil. Some trees that grow near the sea have an alkaline soil, while some grow on a peat soil, which is very acid. The scale for the pH goes from 0 to 14, with a neutral point being pH 7. The soil increases its acidity from pH 7 to 0, and increases its alkalinity from pH 7 to 14. In other words:

• a value of 7 is neutral;
• a value below 7.0 is acid;
• a value above 7.0 is alkaline.

Some other ingredients of your soil mix can be as follows:

• grit: 2 to 6mm, rough or smooth. Rough is preferable. Wash well to remove the dust;
• sand: finer than grit. Should be coarse and angular, not like beach sand, which is far too fine for bonsai;
• organic: rotted pine bark, leaf mold, peat moss and soilless compost;
• loam: a mix comprising a mixture of the above, clay or proprietary brands. It does not mean garden soil.

Japanese and clay-type granule soils are designed to be water-retentive, but to allow free passage of excess water. Hence they will dry out quickly. If this is a concern, mix them with organic material. Some organic materials can compact single soils and cause root rot. Use grit to break them up.

Pines require a soil with a higher grit or sand content. For many years, a normal blend has been 70 percent grit to 30 percent organic. However, Japanese branded imported soils are now used, either on their own or mixed with each other. The problem with this is that although they will retain some water, you must be extra careful about the tree's watering requirements. Your local club, dealer, or expert will guide you.

Descriptive terms commonly associated with certain ranges in soil pH are as follows:

• very acid: 4.5–5.0;
• strongly acid: 5.1–5.5;
• moderately acid: 5.6–6.0;
• slightly acid: 6.1–6.5;
• neutral: 6.6–7.3 (your saliva is 6.6–7.3; blood is 7.3);
• slightly alkaline: 7.4–7.8;
• moderately alkaline: 7.9–8.4 (sea water is 8.2);
• strongly alkaline: 8.5–9.0;
• very strongly alkaline: more than 9.1.

Making the right soil mix will depend on the tree's requirements and your local best practice.

Principles of potting

Here we will look at repotting established and new bonsai material.

Preparation of the pot

Prepare the pot if you are using a different pot for transplanting.

- Make the mesh-retaining clips that will hold the plastic mesh onto the bottom of your pot. The mesh stops the soil from falling through. Start off with a single wire about 6 inches (15 cm) long.
- Bend the wire in two places in opposite directions.
- Bring the bent ends back over the middle of the wire.
- Now bend these ends down. This forms the retainer that goes under the pot, comes up through the mesh and is then bent over.

Put tree-retainer wires or cord through the mesh to hold the bonsai into the pot.

Repotting a bonsai

Repotting is unavoidable as the tree will fill the pot with roots and will then use up all of the soil. Every two to four years, in early to mid-spring, you need to remove some of the roots and then repot the tree so that it gets fresh soil. Young trees need repotting every two years. Old, mature bonsai may only need potting every five years because they are established and slower-growing. In tropical areas, with year-round growth, you may pot more or less frequently at any time of the year, although some places still have optimum times.

- Remove the tree from the pot by using a knife or blunt blade to ease the soil from the edges of the pot.
- Check the soil for insect attack, including root aphid. You can tell the difference between root aphid and the beneficial mycelial fungus that helps roots to grow: mycelium is creamy white, while aphid is bluish white. Aphids can also be seen as little, oval, white, seedlike shapes in the webs that they create, which look similar to mycelium.
- If there are any aphids, remove as many as possible. This is usually fairly easy as the aphid prefers to live near the wall of the pot and so the outer area can be removed.
- Check for mycelium. You can buy mycelium in a kit that contains a number of different varieties of tree mycelium.
- Remove between a third and a half of the old soil.
- Check for damaged or dead roots and remove them. When cutting big roots, seal with bonsai wound-sealer to stop rot and insects. Some growers do not do this, but I feel that it is best to be safe rather than sorry.
- Always keep the roots moist during this time as they can easily dry out.
- Prepare the dry soil by sieving out the fines or dust.
- Mound in the middle of the area that you wish to plant.
- Press down slightly with the tree.
- Fill in the areas with more new soil.
- Tie in the tree, protecting the roots on the surface, if necessary, with rubber- or plastic-padding sheet sections.
- Tap the outside of the pot with a rubber hammer, or the side of your hands, to make sure that the soil gets into all the areas of the roots. Be careful when using a chopstick, or similar, as it can damage the fine roots and cause root rot.

Feeding bonsai

Macronutrients and micronutrients

Rod is an Oregon-certified nursery professional and a former Iowa-certified nurseryman, with a bachelor of science degree in horticulture from Iowa State University and 27 years of experience in orchards, nurseries and landscaping. Rod worked at Dennis' Seven Dees Nursery in Portland, Oregon for 16 years. He now works for Cascadian Nurseries. Rod has a pruning and landscape-design business and teaches home-gardening classes for Portland Community College.

Plant nutrients
by Rod Smith

Plants need water, air, light, a suitable temperature and 16 nutrients to grow. Plants get carbon, hydrogen and oxygen from air and water. The other 13 nutrients come from the soil. Soil nutrients are divided into two groups according to the amounts needed by plants. The macronutrients are nitrogen, phosphorus, potassium, calcium, magnesium and sulfur. The micronutrients, which are needed only in trace amounts, are iron, manganese, boron, zinc, copper, molybdenum and chlorine.

Japanese soil Kiriyu

These nutrients are essential for plant growth. Plants will grow normally until they run short of one nutrient. Then growth is limited by the availability of that nutrient. Occasionally, two or more nutrients will run short at the same time. If the nutrients are deficient, or too abundant, then plants will be discolored or deformed. The deficiency symptoms will indicate which nutrient or nutrients are needed. However, it is much better to supply additional nutrients before deficiency symptoms appear. A soil test will tell which nutrients are low before growth is affected.

Macronutrients

Nitrogen, N, stimulates leaf and stem growth. Nitrogen deficiency causes reduced growth and pale-yellowish-green leaves. The older leaves turn yellowish first since the nitrogen is readily moved from the old leaves to the new growth. If the soil is cold and wet, nitrogen in the soil is not as available to the plants. Excess nitrogen may cause potassium deficiency.

Phosphorus, P, is important in the germination and growth of seeds, the production of flowers and fruit and the growth of roots. Phosphorus deficiency causes reduced growth and small leaves that drop early, starting with the oldest leaves. Leaf color is a dull, bluish green that becomes purplish or bronzed. Leaf edges often turn scorched brown. Excess phosphorus may cause potassium deficiency.

Potassium, K, promotes general vigor, disease resistance and sturdy growth. Potassium deficiency causes stunted growth, with the leaves positioned close together. Starting with the older leaves, the leaf tips and edges turn scorched brown and the leaf edges roll up. Excess potassium may cause calcium and magnesium deficiencies.

Japanese soil

Calcium, Ca, is a major ingredient in cell walls and is important for root growth, especially that of the root tips. Calcium deficiency causes poorly developed roots with weak tips. Leaves are distorted, with hooked tips and curled margins.

Magnesium, Mg, is vital for chlorophyll production, and is important in most enzyme reactions. Magnesium deficiency causes different symptoms in different plants, but commonly includes leaf-yellowing, with brilliant tints. Leaves may suddenly drop off without withering. Symptoms show first on older leaves. Excess magnesium may cause calcium deficiency.

Sulfur, S, is an ingredient in proteins and is necessary for chlorophyll formation. Sulfur deficiency causes slow growth, with small, round leaves that roll upward and are stiff and brittle. Leaves drop off and tip buds die.

Micronutrients

washed grit for good drainage.

Iron, Fe, is necessary for chlorophyll formation and for oxygen transfer. Iron deficiency causes leaf-yellowing, while leaf veins stay green. Younger leaves are affected first. Excess lime may cause iron deficiency.

Manganese, Mn, is a catalyst for many enzymes, and is important for chlorophyll formation. Manganese deficiency causes different symptoms in different plants, but commonly causes leaves to turn yellow, while veins stay green. White or gray specks may appear on leaves. Older leaves are affected first. Excess manganese may cause iron deficiency, and may cause symptoms similar to manganese deficiency.

Boron, B, is necessary for the movement of sugars, for reproduction and for water intake by cells. It also tends to keep calcium in a soluble form. Boron deficiency causes distorted and dead growing tips, hollow stems and deformed fruit. Leaves are often scorched and curled and are sometimes mottled and discolored. Young leaves are affected first. Excess boron may cause scorched leaf edges similar to that caused by potassium or magnesium deficiencies.

Zinc, Zn, is necessary for the production of proteins and affects plant size and maturity. Zinc deficiency causes leaf-yellowing between the veins, usually with purple or dead spots, starting with the older leaves. Leaves are positioned close together, and are small and deformed. Fruiting is reduced. Excess zinc may cause iron deficiency.

Copper, Cu, is necessary for the production of proteins and is also important for reproduction. Copper deficiencies cause bluish-green leaves that may wither or fail to unfold. Younger leaf tips may be yellow at the edges. Growing tips may form rosettes. Excess copper may cause iron deficiency.

Molybdenum, Mo, is essential to nitrate enzymes and for the formation of root nodules in beans and peas. Molybdenum deficiencies cause yellow mottling and dead spots on the leaves. In some plants, the growing tips are distorted or killed.

Chlorine, Cl, may affect carbohydrate metabolism and photosynthesis. Chlorine deficiencies may cause stubby roots and wilting. Excess chlorine may cause leaf edges to scorch in a similar way to that caused by potassium deficiency.

Fertilizing

Most plants in most soils will grow better if additional nutrients are provided by fertilizing. A soil test will give a complete and accurate measure of the nutrients in the soil. A general recommendation is that all soils need more nitrogen. Shallow-rooted plants, such as grass and flowers, need more phosphorus and potassium. Acid-loving plants, such as rhododendrons, azaleas, camellias, junipers and pin oaks, often need more iron. Sometimes sandy soils need micronutrients, but rarely clay soils. Certain micronutrients may be deficient in certain parts of the country. Boron is sometimes deficient in America's Pacific Northwest, for example.

Many fertilizers are available to supply additional nutrients. Some fertilizers only supply one nutrient. Many supply N, P and K only. A few fertilizers include all of the macronutrients and micronutrients. The label on the package will indicate which nutrients are included, as well as the sources of the nutrients. The nutrients are identical, whether they come from organic or synthetic sources, but the source will affect how quickly the nutrients are available to plants. Ammonia sulfate and water-soluble fertilizers release most of their nitrogen in a few days, and may burn plants if too much is applied. Blood meal releases its nitrogen over a period of months. Organic fertilizers and specially treated synthetic fertilizers release their nutrients slowly, so they last longer and will not burn. Deeper-rooted trees and shrubs can be fertilised once a year, but shallow-rooted plants, such as grass and flowers, will need regular fertilizing throughout the growing season.

Water can move nitrogen several centimeters in the soil. Nitrogen applied in the fall may be carried too deep into the soil by winter rains. February or March is the best time to feed trees and shrubs. Phosphorus and potassium hardly move in the soil. To get them down to tree roots, punch a hole in the soil with a bar, or use a root-feeder and inject them 12 inches (30 cm) deep every 24 inches (60 cm) in rings from the trunk to twice the length of the branches. The feeder roots are found throughout the area under and around a tree, not just at the drip line.

Rod Smith

Products that contain micronutrients

Micronutrients are supplied in special micronutrient packages (such as MicroMax, STEM, Apex Micronutrient Package and others), which bind readily to organic matter if used in conjunction with soilless mixes.

The micronutrient mix is sprinkled on the surface of dry soil and then watered in. It will increase the acidity of the soil temporarily and is best applied when repotting, or once a year in spring, at bud break.

Washed horticultural grit.

Feeding

Bonsai will need feeding if you use the single-soil approach as they cannot live on water alone. Feeding is easy, and here is a breakdown of feeds and the basic regime.

A high-nitrogen feed makes the leaves grow.

A low-nitrogen feed makes the branches, roots and cambium (under-bark) grow. Tomato fertilizer is also low in nitrogen. I advocate the use of a low-nitrogen feed with such soft-leaved trees as maples in the early flush of growth as it helps the leaves to become stronger. Use it in the later part of the year, just prior to fall or in the winter season in colder climes.

0.10.10, or similar, is a zero-nitrogen feed. This is used with most conifers at the beginning of the season and through the early stages of bud or candle development.

Acid-loving plants: use Miracid, or similar (preferred by azaleas, satsukis, ericas and stewartia).

For young trees or trees that are being initially styled

Spring: use at half-strength when the buds are open — 0.10.10.
Build to full strength in late spring and use high nitrogen after the first flush of growth.
Feed half-strength through most of the growing season in hotter areas.

Summer: if in a hot area, do not fertilize. If in a cool area, stop in midsummer. The trees cannot absorb fertilizer at this time: they go into semi-dormancy because of the heat and stop growing.

Fall: reduce to half-strength and only use a low-nitrogen fertilizer. This helps the bonsai into the main dormant season in cooler climes.

Brand names popular in America and the UK differ from those in Australia or South Africa. In general, it is fine to use popular houseplant food, but not lawn or grass food because it is far too high in nitrogen and can easily damage the roots.

General: Miracle-Gro, Baby Bio, Peters.
Specific recipes in different forms: Chempack is a UK-based fertilizer, which I have seen sold in other countries.

Surface cakes to lie on the soil and release their nutrients slowly: Green King, Bio Gold, Rapeseed Cake surface dressing.

Low nitrogen: 0.10.10, tomato fertilizer, Tomorite and other brands. Low nitrogen encourages development of the branches and roots in bonsai, which is why it is important at the very start of the growing season and toward the end.

Special: Miracid (for acid lovers)

For mature trees

I suggest that surface pellet feeds, such as Rapeseed Cake or Bio Gold, are the best option. The direct feeding of liquid fertilizers through the soil should be no more than between two and four times a year when a bonsai is mature. Too much feeding will generate lush growth. Adding trace elements is, however, important. In all cases, when dealing with older trees, less is more.

Pests and diseases

An ant home. Ants can cause problems for bonsai.

Outdoor bonsai will attract a range of pests, such as greenfly, weevils, ants, slugs, caterpillars, scale and wasps, which munch old, fissured bark for their nests. Both indoor and outdoor bonsai suffer from blackfly, mites, woodworm, and whitefly. The pests that you will find depend on which part of the world you live in. However, wherever you are, healthy trees will remain healthy when they are checked daily.

Systemic insecticides are slow-acting, but successful. Systemic applications go in through the roots and come out through the entire bonsai — bark, branches and leaves.

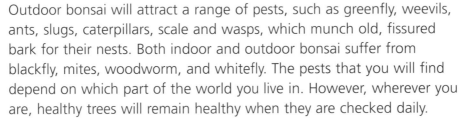

Don't allow cones to form as they draw strength from the tree.

Foliar insecticides are sprayed onto the leaves and needles. They are very quick-acting. Not all bonsai can take foliar chemicals though, so read the instructions. They usually list the trees and plants that you cannot use that chemical on.

Caterpillars are real pests.

Trunk and branch washes are winter sprays that will act on over-wintering pests.

Fungicides are used in a powder form and mixed with water. Powder is safer than the liquid form, which is still available in some countries. Use for fungal problems, but avoid contact with the soil of pines.

Lopho-Lophodermium pinastre **needle cast has yellow bands and brown edges.**

Cocktails are a mix of feed and insecticide to cut down on spraying twice.

Rot signals are fungus spores of different colors.

Specifics are insecticides for specific problems, such as vine weevil.

I cannot cover every insect or disease here, and your local nurseries will tell you the best specific insecticide for your part of the world. There are many brand names, and the same chemical changes its name in different countries, so the information given here is, by default, general.

Organic pest control

There are a number of specialist companies around the world that supply organic pest-control materials. This website is a good place to start as it offers a wide range of suitable products: http://www.extremelygreen.com

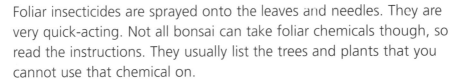

Don't prune out larch during the growing season, but only in winter.

The organic countermeasures listed on page 38 will get you started, but ask your local garden center for advice on other available options.

Fungus growth can be seen on the trunk of this *Lonicera***.**

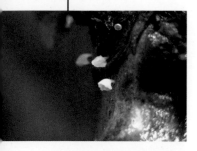

Fungus indicates when
conditions are too wet.

Aphid damage.

Coral spot on a juniper caused
by too much dampness.

An aphid midge.

A venomous red-back
spider. Spiders will eat
pests for you.

38

Lime sulfur spray

Neat lime sulfur is used as a preservative and whitener of dead-wood areas for bonsai; diluted, it can also act as an organic pest control.

Lime sulfur is an insecticide/fungicide that protects against a variety of pests, including scales, mites and borer insects. It is also a control for such diseases as powdery mildew, anthracnose, rust, some galls, some leaf curls and black spot.

Lime sulfur is applied during the dormant (winter) season and in the early spring period, just before growth starts, and is sprayed onto affected areas. It smothers overwintering fungi, insect eggs and disease-causing viruses.

Beneficial parasites and nematodes

I first came across beneficial parasites and nematodes during the early 1980s, and they have now become a staple means of pest control. In many cases, they act as a preventative, as well as a cure.

Aphid parasitoids (*A. matricariae*)

Aphid parasitoids are tiny (2 to 3 mm), stingless mini-wasps. They help to prevent and correct low-level aphid populations. You can let them work together with other predatory insects to control over forty aphid species.

The way that these wasps control the aphid population is a little gory. The wasps lay their eggs in the aphids. The eggs hatch and the grubs devour the aphids from within.

It is advisable to use *A. matricariae* to stop aphid infestations as soon as they are noticed. Use them as a control or preventative measure for light to medium infestations of aphids. *A. matricariae* will work with most of the common aphid species.

Aphid midges (*A. aphidimyza*)

Aphid midges are about 3 mm long. Aphid-midge larvae are hunters. They can control large populations of over sixty species of aphids. The aphid midge can travel longish distances and will actively seek out aphids, even high up in trees.

The midges are sent to you as cocoons, which soon hatch into adult insects. The midges mate, find some aphids and lay their eggs. The eggs hatch into small, orange larvae, which devour the aphids from within.

Ladybugs (*Hippodamia convergens*)

The familiar ladybird, or ladybug, is a predator that feeds on aphids at any opportunity. They are generally recognized as the best control for aphids.

The adult beetles will seek out and eat aphids. The female ladybird can lay up to fifty eggs per day. They will usually lay these orange, football-shaped eggs on the upper sides of leaves on infested plants. The eggs hatch into black, alligatorlike larvae with orange markings. The larvae are also extremely active in looking out for, and eating, aphids.

**Wasps and yellow jackets
process dead wood,
including shari.**

Beneficial nematodes (Hb/Sf)

The Hb nematodes work their way into the soil to a depth of around 7 inches (18 cm) and search out the slow-moving grubs, such as beetle grubs and chafers, that inhabit the deeper layers of the soil. All nematodes like warm soil; when the soil temperature drops below 68°F (20°C), they become less effective.

The Sf nematodes will stay in the top 1 to 3 inches (2.5–7.5 cm) of soil. Both species act by invading grubs or larval bodies and releasing bacteria that are deadly to the grubs or larvae. Death usually occurs between 24 and 48 hours later. Nematodes can produce up to three generations of themselves during the following three weeks, and they will live until the grub or larvae infestation has been reduced.

There are nematodes that can handle vine weevil, and with the rise in vine-weevil infestations, this is one way to fight this pest organically.

Garlic concentrate for plants

Garlic concentrate for plants can be used in areas that attract mosquitoes, gnats, deer flies and other pests relating to humans, pets and livestock. The key to using garlic effectively is to apply it to plants before a pest problem arises.

**Aphids can be a terrible pest on
deciduous trees and conifers.**

Millipedes

I like millipedes. I love the way that they curl up and are not slimy. However, it is better not to have them in your bonsai or penjing garden.

Certain millipedes, such the spotted-snake millipede (*Blaniulus guttulatus*), are serious garden pests because they attack the roots and other parts of plants. During periods of drought, these attacks are more prevalent, and it is thought that the millipedes attack the plant principally for the moisture content. Once plants have been damaged, however, the resultant decay of the damaged tissues means that the millipedes now have a food source.

In the wild, millipedes are very useful because they recycle dead and decaying plants back into the soil.

Control is rarely necessary. If required, it should primarily involve moisture control because these arthropods are susceptible to drying out.

**Aphid excretia, or waste, can
suffocate buds.**

There is a larval beetle known as a millipede-killer that specializes in feeding on millipedes. These beetle larvae bore into the side of the millipede's body and suck out the fluids. All that remains after the larva has completed its feeding orgy is the hollow shell of the millipede!

Moss

Remember to remove some of the moss on the surface of your soil in the winter as it can harbor pests. Plant the moss in a separate tray and treat it with a systemic. It will be ready to reapply in spring. Protect the moss from birds by placing plastic mesh over it. Otherwise, collect or cultivate fresh moss, but check for insects before applying it.

**Foliage and insects go
together. You're not immune.**

Pruning and trimming.

Pruning

Pruning is part of the design process and falls into two areas: pruning to develop ramification, or twig structure, and pruning to develop shape.

Pruning to develop ramification is done to both conifers and leafed trees. Cutting back long branches forces the tree to bud back along the wood and so develop new growth. That is left to grow and is, in turn, cut back, and so the cycle continues.

Pruning to develop shape is done at the initial stages, in order to design the rough outline, and then toward the end to define the shape and remove extraneous growth. Cutting back in the midsummer, dormant period in temperate to cooler climates is also a method used to define the shape of the bonsai.

Use sharp tools and sterilize them after each use by running them under boiling water. Apply a little machine oil to keep metal tools from rusting. Clean tools are essential to reduce the possibility of passing disease from one plant to another.

Stainless-steel tools, such as those made by Joshua Roth, are much easier to keep clean. Although I like to use one particular make, you will find dealers everywhere selling varying qualities of bonsai tools. I always suggest that you get what you pay for.

The most important pruning tip that I can give you is always to seal the cuts afterward. You need to help the trees to heal and protect the cuts from further damage. I have seen too many die-backs from rough pruning when the cut has not been sealed.

Use the right tool for the cut. Using light shears for branch cutting will damage both the shears and the branch. Be aware of saw-cut overlap. When you use a saw to remove a branch, the blade may cut over the intended area and cause damage on a different part of the tree. Carry Band-Aids or Elastoplasts in your tool kit. You will, at some stage, cut yourself!

Wiring and shaping

Wiring is the principal means of creating a bonsai shape. When the tree has set into its new shape, the wire is cut off.

Wire comes in a number of sizes, ranging from 1 to 6 mm in thickness. The easiest wire to use is anodized aluminum, preferably in a brown or copper color. The softer aluminum is good for deciduous trees and detail wiring, where strength and rigidity are less vital.

Copper wire comes as annealed wire in coils. When applied, it hardens into shape and holds the plant in the correct position. This hardening is caused by the structure of the copper, which introduces dislocations into the molecules. The dislocations reduce the softness of the annealed wire, which means that it is not easily bent again, once worked. As copper wire is much more rigid when bent than aluminum wire, you need smaller-sized wire. I worked out that as copper wire is between two and three times stronger *pro rata* than aluminum, you need a size half or a third less than aluminum. I also use copper wire in pairs and multiples along the branch as this allows neat application and easy spurring-off for twigs without damaging the branches. In fact, I now prefer copper to aluminum because it is easy to bend and then hardens into shape.

Wiring techniques

Branch-wiring

The wire controls the way in which the branch is growing, so it is important to make sure that the wire does not wobble about.

- Measure the wire about a third longer than the branches to allow for loss of length in the wiring process.
- Anchor the wire to another branch. Make sure that it goes in opposite directions to stop the wobble effect.
- Anchor the wire to the trunk. This technique is used on slimmer trees. Be careful not to mark the trunk.
- Always wire in the same direction and do not cross wires as that will force wire into the trunk and cause scarring. It is also untidy.
- Remove wires before they bite into the bark.

Using turnbuckle techniques to move heavy branches.

To bend very thick branches, tie long lengths of wire for strength.

Wrapping a branch in vet tape. I developed this technique in Atlanta.

Here you can see the lengths of wire waiting to be shaped into the branch.

Vet wrap is better than raffia, and because it sticks to itself, it does not damage bark.

Vet tape wrapped around wire holds the wire tightly in place.

Self-amalgamating tape. Before extreme bending, wrap branches with a cotton bandage.

A close-up view of the wire and vet wrap.

Most conifer branches do not need protection when wiring.

A close-up of the wire and vet wrap when applied as multiple wiring.

Fine-wiring buds.

Part of the wire is digging into the branch.

Single wiring.

Multiple wiring.

Simple wiring

You must ensure that the wire is taken to the tips of every branch as that controls the entire direction, and not just a part of it.

Technical wiring

Technical wiring is used for special control techniques, such as bringing down a branch. It may be preferable to wiring the entire branch.

- Always make sure that the lower branch is stronger than the top one if the upper branch needs to be pulled down. Apply the wire around both branches and slip in protection pads on each branch to prevent damage.
- Insert a small pencil, a piece of thicker wire or a twig and twist the wires.
- As they tighten, the upper branch is pulled down.
- Alternatively, use a turnbuckle to lever the branches.

Multiple wiring

I developed my multiple-wiring technique to reduce the time that it took me to wire branches. Although it is very easy for beginners, and reduces wiring time by about 50 percent, it is not a traditional wiring method. I was trained in the traditional Japanese methods of wiring, which generally use two — and

Make sure that the wires are anchored well.

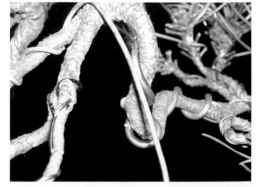

Only wire the branch that you wish to bend, not everything.

sometimes three — wires to reduce the amount of thick wire needed. Two wires are slightly stronger than one, and you have more control. I extended this concept to use up to ten wires. I use the thinner wires together. They act like a thick wire, but with the advantage that they can be spurred off onto twigs and other branches on the area that I am wiring. The technique is suitable only for the initial styling of any tree. Beginners like multiple wiring because it is quick, neat and easy to do.

Some tips:
- use wires of different thicknesses for multiple wiring;
- anchor the wire well at the start of a branch so as not to move the base of the wire up to the twigs;
- spur off one of the wires onto each of the twigs.

Heavy-branch-wiring

In this technique, the branch has to be protected from damage before it is bent. Raffia is the most common of the bark-protection materials. It is soaked in ice-cold water before being applied. When the raffia dries, it tightens onto the wood. The main problem with raffia is that when it is removed, it can also take the bark off. Never apply raffia to old, fissured bark as that will damage it.

Self-amalgamating rubber tape is stronger and more protective than raffia. It is useful when bending really big branches 1 to 6 inches (2.5–15 cm) in diameter. The tape stretches with the branch, and this flexibility makes it more suitable than raffia. You must protect the bark with cotton or a bandage to stop the tape from adhering to the wood.

I discovered stretch vet tape by accident a few years back, when I was in the United States. I was speaking in Georgia at one of my favorite clubs, the Atlanta Bonsai Club, and needed to demonstrate wiring techniques. I remembered using an adhering stretch support bandage for my ankle, and thought that it might do the job. The bandage was like paper, with stretchy elastic stitched in many rows through it. I went to a pharmacy and found a small roll of this medical-grade material. The resultant literati pine demonstrated my points, but looked a little odd wrapped in a pink bandage!

A friend of mine who owns a horse told me about vet wrap, which is used to wrap horses' fetlocks. Not only is it a fraction of the price of medical-grade stretch support, but it also comes in many colors and in different widths. I had found my alternative to raffia and began demonstrating its benefits to the bonsai community all over

Wiring is the most important element in delivering a design.

Pulling down a branch using a tourniquet technique.

Raffia is used to protect branches.

Wire only the part of the branch that needs shaping.

Self-amalgamating plumber's tape.

To avert damage, always protect the tree when heavy-wire-bending.

the world. Since then, it has become a popular part of most growers' tool kits. In my demo piece using a Hinkoki cypress (*Chamaecyparis obtuse*), you will see that I use vet wrap extensively.

How long does the wire stay on?

Three months is the general guideline for leaving wire on.

Young trees

No more than three months. The places of vigorous growth include the top, or apex, and the ends, or tips, of the branches. Check after six weeks to make sure that the wire is not biting in. Do not unwire, as you may damage developing buds, but snip off the wire carefully.

Older or mature trees

The apex and the tips of branches will grow faster and so will need constant checks after the first four to six weeks. The species of tree will determine the length of time that the wire stays on.

Slower-growing trees

Pines (*Pinus*), junipers (*Juniperus*) and yews (*Taxus*) have fast-growing foliage. However, the trunk and branches grow more slowly, so wire can be left on for six months to over a year in temperate climates. However, it will need to be removed sooner in warmer areas, where the growth is generally more vigorous. In any climate, the tips and apical areas will still need to be checked every week in the growing period to watch for wire biting in. The main branches are usually slower to grow than the tips, and wire can be left for longer here.

Faster-growing trees

Maples (*Acer*) and elms (*Ulmus*) will need constant checking after three weeks. Remove the wire as soon as you see the branches expanding into it. Spend a few minutes each day with your trees.

Removal of the wire

I have seen new buds and soft bark destroyed when growers unwind the wire to save a little money. Why spend all of that time developing ramification of your foliage only to destroy the very thing that you set out to do? The best way is to cut the wire carefully from the entire branch so that it does not damage the tree. Although wire is not cheap, you do get a lot of it for your money, so balance the cost of cutting off the wire against saving essential parts of your bonsai.

How to view a bonsai

When you first grow a bonsai, you will come across the term "front of the bonsai." In the creation of a bonsai, there is generally a better viewing angle, which is sometimes called the front. This viewing point is the starting point for a bonsai. In some cases, the best viewing angle is determined by the best surface root, or nebari. Of course, a tree growing in nature does not have a front, but anyone looking at that tree will have a favorite viewing angle. In fact, every person that looks at the same tree may prefer a different viewing angle, or "front." Making a bonsai requires some formal discipline, so a bonsai designer chooses a front. But as a bonsai designer, I would like to emphasize that concentrating on a front may have detrimental artistic implications for the bonsai as a whole.

Front A: you need a preferred viewing point.

Front B: but that is also determined by the structure.

Certainly, there needs to be a front, but there should also be a back, a right side, a left side and a top (looking down through the foliage) to make sure that the branches are not covering each other completely, a surface-root image and, of course, a hidden view — a good underground root system. Roots will mirror the branches because, in normal circumstances, each branch is fed by a particular root.

Front C: good nebari; branch placement comes into this "front."

Front D: or a feeling may determine your own preferred view. I would either remove or elevate the sticking-out branch.

chapter 2
evolving into a bonsai

This chapter looks at the real art of bonsai: what it takes to create a bonsai and what you need to know about looking after it once you have completed that miniature image. We will look at the general species care for pine.

Workshops and demonstrations

Windswept styles

The windswept image is probably one of the most difficult images to deliver. It is easy to slant a group of trees and to say that they are windswept, but unless it really feels as though the wind is pushing the trees along its path, the image does not work. It's about emotion, about energy and about understanding nature. You should almost feel that force and shiver.

Paperbarks (*Melaleuca*) are native to Australia. When I was staying with Dianne Boekhout in Perth, she showed me some trees that she had collected. They were great — very tender, but well worth the collection. Paperbarks are water loving trees that like their roots to be near a water source. I found a large slab and we simply placed the two elements together to create a windswept group overhanging a river. Dianne's images of *Melaleuca* in nature were my inspiration.

Australian paperbarks were my design inspiration.

Paperbarks grow near water.

Paperbark (*Melaleuca rhaphiophylla*) yamadori.

The first tree is placed. Dianne Boekhout and Syd Reeves assist.

The group is designed as if overhanging a river.

Syd helps to secure the trees and finish off the surface.

Soil and moss arrangement.

The paperbark group after its styling.

The paperbark group: my front.

Using a slab as part of the design

Don DeLuca, Australia

Don DeLuca is a great bonsai-grower. Full of energy and enthusiasm, he brought this heavy, 6-foot-long (2 m) stone slab planted in a fairly full manner with a particular variety of *Parrotia persica*, which has a small, red-edged leaf. Don has been developing these quite rare trees at his nursery. Although the slab was fully planted, Don wanted me to insert another, larger tree into the main group. I suggested that it would be better to dismantle the entire thing and allow me to redesign the image for his workshop. Don removed the trees and we replanted all of them in a tighter mass at one side. I wanted to show him that the slab had now become part of the design instead of just acting as a large pot. The split image that had been a case of divide and fall now became a powerful, windswept image with great integrity, using the slab as part of the design and not just as a base.

Don DeLuca brought this large slab planted with *Parrotia persica* for the workshop.

We replanted the trees, creating a more dynamic image.

Windswept juniper group

Lindsay Muirhead, New Zealand

Styling a windswept image into a bonsai requires some knowledge of how nature forces trees into a slanting position. In these workshops, I wanted to give the feeling of huge pressure from wind. Although the material may not be good individually, when used as a group the sheer force of the image can illustrate the forces of nature. Lindsay Muirhead is a New Zealand artist who paints landscapes of outstanding beauty. I am the proud owner of one of his paintings, and cannot help but desire more. That is like collecting bonsai. You get one and then want more. In this case, the trees were very sparse, but very strong. In the workshop, I asked Lindsay to remove all of the trees and to clean out the roots carefully, without cutting anything. We needed to apply a simple design to give the illusion of the force, pressure and speed of wind. This is how the eye perceives the object, and the design meant resiting the existing trees at an angle to one side, as if pushed. I think that it works, and while there is not much tree material, it's a case of less is more. The other two images are of trees in Lindsay's native New Zealand to provide inspiration: a group of windswept, thin tea trees (*Leptospermum*) on the side of a cliff and windswept totaras on North Island, near an old volcanic cone.

Lindsay Muirhead's juniper group was static.

Windswept totara.

Now it is a windswept image with dynamic movement.

Windswept tea trees (*Leptospermum*).

Juniperus chinensis styling

Junipers (*Juniperus*) need the same growing conditions as pines (*Pinus*) in most cases. The difference is in the development of the growth. New tip growth on the ends of the foliage of junipers needs pinching out. This will encourage back-budding and the subsequent thickening of growth in the areas that have been pinched out. At some stage, the growth may need to be cut back hard to force inner growth and growth nearer to the trunk, if that is part of your design.

In this demonstration, we see the first styling to get the image in place. The follow-up period is the crucial part of the development. It is a lot of work keeping a juniper, but the rewards are worth it. This is garden-center material that had a difficult twin trunk. After wiring and shaping, two became one. I had created the style and now added a slight tilt or slant to the tree, giving it a slightly windblown appearance as opposed to a fully windswept one. A touch of movement: less is more!

Before the first *Juniperus chinensis* styling.

After the first *Juniperus chinensis* styling. A slight slant creates a windblown aspect.

Cedar windswept group

Ric Roberts, Australia

This very large group had no structure, perhaps because it was so large. The heights of the trees were causing problems, and Ric needed to break it up and start again. I wanted more energy from the trees, and had to reset the group twice before I got what I was looking for. Although the trees are still tall, the final design makes a very strong, windswept image.

The cedar group prior to being styled. This was a very tall group.

The group was dismantled and reset.

The completed cedar group, wired and styled by Ric Roberts and Craig Coussins.

Pines (*Pinus*): understanding the species for bonsai

These are general techniques that I have found to be successful, and that can be applied to many species within the requirements of the pine (*Pinus*) genus.

Goyomatsu: white pine (*Pinus parviflora*) created by Kunio Kobayashi.

White pine

White-pine bonsai, the most popular of the material sold as bonsai, come from many places – China, Japan, Korea and even Israel. However, they mostly come from the Asian Pacific Rim area. Despite the huge number of varieties, or cultivars, of white pine, all have a white stomatic band down the middle of the needle (or leaf). The tree, or shrub, in its original state is a blue-green color, but cultivars can be any color from green to bright yellow. The needles are 2 to 4 inches (5–7 cm) long. The cones, which are formed from the flowers, are around 3 to 5 inches (7–12 cm) long, conical in shape and can be in clusters or singles. In bonsai cultivation, we can reduce the needles to a size smaller than 1/2 inch (1.2 cm), although the normal size is about 1 inch (2.5 cm). Imported trees are often styled very simply, with a twist or two in the trunk, and are usually grafted onto a stronger, black-pine base. Some varieties have short needle clusters and some, very dense needle clusters. All are *Pinus parviflora*, although in Europe, this species is also called *Pinus pentaphylla*, followed by the cultivar name. The difference between white pine and other pine species is that white pine has a cluster of five needles around each bud. The Scots, red and black pines have needle clusters of two, and some varieties of red have clusters of three. Its natural growth habit is low and conical when young, but flat-topped and spreading when the tree is mature. As a bonsai, it can be any shape, but the common style is pyramidal, with the

branches growing in clearly defined steps up to the apex, or tip, of the tree. This creates an image of a younger tree, but as a bonsai, it is much more attractive to the viewer.

If you buy a white pine, make sure that you find out about its requirements. Many bonsai die within a few weeks of purchase if they are not kept correctly. This is sad, as a bonsai really requires very little in the way of care.

- Keep the pine out of extreme weather conditions — wind, rain and sun — and also centrally heated homes.
- Put the tree in a slightly shaded place and spray it lightly every day for the first 14 days. After a couple of weeks, give the tree about four hours of sun per day, but still find it a place away from high winds.
- It is wiser not to feed a new bonsai immediately. Wait until the tree has settled down. The tree may have been repotted recently and the roots freshly cut. If you feed it too soon after purchasing it, you may damage the roots. Ask when the tree was last repotted. Explain why you need this information. If the seller is not sure, it is best to withhold feeding for around six weeks.
- If you get, or buy, a tree in the winter, do not bring the bonsai into a centrally heated house as this will aggravate the normal growing period of the tree, exhausting it, and will dry up the needles.

Watering

Pines need semidry conditions in the winter and the soil kept slightly damp in the growing season. Pine bonsai do not like very wet conditions. Only spray the needles from summer to early fall, but in both the morning and late evening.

Needle reduction

Reduce the size of the needles as follows.

- To reduce needles on established trees, start to withhold water as the buds develop. This makes the needles smaller. When the buds have set and the needles have opened, resume normal watering. (Note: this is not appropriate for young trees.)
- Needle reduction can also be encouraged by plucking the candles in the right order, thus promoting new growth along the branches. This can be achieved on old wood that has not fissured up. Reduction of the branch tips can also force newer and smaller buds.
- Too much feeding, the wrong soil and too much watering will make the needles grow large. It's a fine balance, and one that is easily learned. Less is more!

Pests and diseases

Pines are prone to aphids, adelgids, mealy bugs, red spider mites, and *Lophodermium pinastre* (pine-needle cast), or "Lopho." If pests arrive, treat them with a systemic insecticide.

Adelgids look like a wooly fluff between the needles. These small, aphid-like insects are always associated with conifers. They are not woolly aphids, but have their own family (Adelgidae) within the insect order Homoptera. They are closely related to the woolly aphids (Eriosomatidae) and the Phylloxeran aphids (Phylloxeridae). Adelgids are also known for producing woolly masses and/or galls on the host plant. Whether they feed on needles and stems, through the bark or within galls, depends on the species of conifer involved. Many adelgid species have alternative host plants, where specific life stages develop. Damage to plants can range from aesthetic to killing the host plant. Systemic insecticide will kill adelgids. Use a concentrated hose spray to wash away the fluff or a soft toothbrush if infestation is minor.

Lopho is identified by lateral yellow stripes on the pine needles. It is a fungus, and is treated with a copper fungicide in a weekly dose for five or six weeks. (Note: when using any fungicide on a pine, do not allow it to get onto the soil. Cover the soil with a polythene sheet or plastic bag and then with a towel. Fungicide will damage the beneficial mycelium fungus that helps the pine roots to grow.)

Feeding pines

Feed pines as follows.
- Always use bought fertilizers at half strength.
- Young trees: in the spring, feed with a high-nitrogen fertilizer; in summer, with a balanced fertilizer; and in early fall, with a low-nitrogen fertilizer. Feed every three weeks at the beginning of the season and every four weeks by early summer through to the end of fall.
- Established trees: using fertilizers at full strength is particularly dangerous as the roots are very tender and may suffer from being fed. You do not want lush juvenile growth, so feed until early summer with low-nitrogen fertilizer. Feed balanced feed in summer, and in fall, feed with low-nitrogen fertilizer again.
- Feed maturing trees approximately every five weeks using slow-release fertilizer pellets, such as Bio Gold. Mature trees need just enough feed to replace lost nutrients in the soil. Feeding trace elements is necessary for all bonsai, but as most proprietary feeds have these in the formula, it is not necessary to add more. Check out this point, of course. When the tree has fully matured into its style, feeding can be as little as two or three times a year, or you can use surface pellet feed.

A black pine (*Pinus thunbergii*) created by Kunio Kobayashi. This tree won the Prime Minister's Award at the prestigious Sakufu10 event in Japan.

Recovery of an old Scots-pine bonsai

Craig Coussins

This tree had a sad story. Once a beautiful tree, it was left in the care of a nursery. The owners neglected it to the extent that, when I returned after a year or so, a major branch had died and I was left with the apex and one branch very low down. I fed it well for two years and brought the vigor back by cutting the candles by half when they became long. That forced new growth along the old wood of the branch. This made the tree dense, but now it needed a styling. Trevor Smith assisted me.

The tree is a Scots pine about seventy years old. The back needles needed to be removed and last year's left on. Wiring up the tree, we started the design with the lower branch and then created a defined apex. It may have to have the top removed and the entire tree may become a "7" shape if this does not work. That is what being a bonsai artist is all about — constant changes until it becomes "right."

The front of the Scots pine.

The left side.

The right side.

The back.

The Scots pine's old needles were removed.

Removing the Scots pine's old needles.

Wiring to the tips.

Elevating the tips.

The new pad.

The new pad again.

Another view of the new pad.

The rough apex.

The Scots pine's old needles have been removed.

The wired-up tree.

The Scots pine pictured after its initial restyle.

Two-year-old needles were carefully cut away, leaving last year's and this year's needles.

The restyled Scots pine from a different angle.

The restyled Scots pine pictured in profile.

55

Pruning pines

Prune the old, two-year-old needles on young trees, and three-year-old needles on mature trees, at the rear of each bud needle cluster every three years. Leave the needles nearer the new buds. Cut the needles above the tiny sheath. Doing this encourages new buds to develop on the older wood.

- Leave only two or three buds at each tip, depending on the health of the tree.
- If you wish to develop young inner buds along the branch, prune out some of the leading tips that are not required.
- Start cutting candles (buds) from the top of the tree by half to two-thirds. Each week, work your way down until you reach the bottom layer of branches.
- The strongest bud at the top of the tree will grow.
- Do not cut all of the buds up and down the tree at the same time as this would exhaust the tree.
- Every three years, it is better to pull the soft, new needles out from the sheath as this will force the tree to create shorter needles the following year.

Pine bud-cutting. The long growth needs to be cut.

Scots pines and other two-needle pines

When Scots pines (*Pinus sylvestris*) are collected or bought from garden centers, they invariably have long branches, with little or no twig structure. The technique for back-budding to develop twigs is quite straightforward.

- From May until June, the tree grows candles. Starting at the bottom of the tree, or the weaker, lower branches, pluck out 50 percent of the candle with your fingers. Hold the bottom of the candle to prevent it from being broken off the tree and pull the rest with your other hand. Leave all obviously weak buds alone. If the branch has only weak buds, wait until they have swollen. If this has not occurred by the second week in June or late spring, then get on with the other branches.
- A week later, pluck the next layer of branches in the same way and work your way up to the, by now vigorous, top area. Using both hands, hold the base of the bud and pluck 50 percent of the balance as you did before.

Pine bud-cutting. This is late in being cut.

The reason for doing this on Scots pines and, indeed, on all two-needle pines, is that the stronger growth is at the top of the tree, so should you start to pluck there, all of the tree's energy would go to that point to repair the damage, bypassing the weaker areas. This could result in eventual loss within the weaker areas.

Pine bud-cutting

Essentially, when the first main bud grows long, cut that in half. If there is a second bud growing, wait until that also becomes long, and then cut it in half and remove the initial bur. This encourages back-budding and fast growth during the year.

If you have been reading this carefully, you will have noticed that the method for two-needle pines differs from that for the white pine, where you start at the top instead of the bottom (see page 51). The tree is then less likely to abort its weaker, lower branches. The white pine has a very specialized series of auxin channels, or flow lines, that require the stronger buds to be trimmed first. The new growth is much softer than that of two-needle pines and, unlike theirs, can be pruned back quite hard after the needles have broken. (Feel the difference between the needle varieties, and you will see what I mean.)

Plucking buds

The next thing to look out for is the formation of twin buds. Pluck the longer bud and wait until the smaller bud has grown longer than the plucked bud.

- Remove the first bud.
- Reduce the new bud by half, but in the same weekly regime.
- At no time leave more than two buds on any growth point. You must reduce this multiple growth to one or two buds if they are important to your overall plan.
- After these new buds have developed, keep the end of that branch short or the sap will bypass the new bud to feed the strongest bud.
- You can remove the entire leader bud if you have strong back buds, but be very careful if these buds are weak or you run the risk of losing the entire branch or twig if you remove the leader.

Pine bud-cutting. Fast back-bud growth.

Pine bud-cutting. Flowers growing on a pine.

Established trees

Once you have established the tree and reduced the needles and so on, you can remove 75 percent of the length of the candles to maintain and build dense pads. This applies to two-needled pines and white pines.

- Look at the inner buds on each branch, and when bud-plucking starts, pluck the inner buds first.
- Five days later, pluck the outer buds.
- Start on the next, upper layer a week later.

Although this increases the actual plucking time by 75 percent, you will soon see the difference. You will see that your tree starts to shape up over the next three or four years.

Maintenance pruning of buds is done when the tree has been relatively completed. Although similar in technique, it goes back to the basic plucking by working on one layer of branches at a time, covering all of the buds at the same time on each layer and progressing upward each week.

Soil type

Speak to the seller of the bonsai, or to other growers in your area, and they will advise you on the best soil for your climate.

- A free-draining soil is important for all pines.
- Trees in hotter climates may need a little more organic material in order to retain moisture than trees in colder or wetter climates.
- If you have access to Japanese soils, a technique for mature trees is to mix 50 percent Akadama with 50 percent Kureyu pine soil for fast drainage, but slight water retention, to avoid sodden conditions.
- Usually repot every three years for young trees and every five years for mature trees.
- Use rust, brown, gray or deep-blue pots for pines.

Light and shade requirements

Blend the light requirements, and you will have a healthy tree.

- Pines like some shade for part of the day in the summer.
- A light area, free from winter climatic problems, is ideal during the cold months.
- Full sun will make the tree more yellow in most cases, while full shade (not advised) will force the glaucous, blue-green color to come out.

Craig defines a Mugho mountain pine (*Pinus mugho*)

I first made this tree from collected material and gave it to my friends Trevor and Faye Yerbury, the international photographers whose work frequently adorns my bonsai books. The tree was now a bit overgrown and needed repotting and some styling. I was never very happy with its inverse taper, and always considered removing one trunk and developing the rest.

When I am at home in Scotland, Trevor Smith, a bonsai artist who I am coaching, comes up to see me a couple of times a year from England and we work on some material. This project was pure wiring and styling. We recovered the shape and styled the branches into lines and form, but the trunk was still a problem. On the previous weekend, I had removed a large jin from a yamadori Scots pine (see page 54), and I realized that it was about the same size as the trunk area of this *Pinus mugho*. I attached the section to the trunk by gluing it and then screwing it with a noncorrosive, brass screw. This solved the inverse problem, much to the delight of both Trevor Smith and Trevor Yerbury.

The mountain pine before its defining.

The back.

The side. Trevor Smith will help me to remove the old needles.

All parts will be wired.

Making pads.

Defining the shape.

Bending twigs into shape.

The defined mountain pine.

The front.

Refining the apex.

The inverse-taper problem.

A treated jin was glued and screwed on.

The final image after repotting (no roots were cut).

Some tools and accessories

A steel root hook is essential for repotting.

The Ken Moore turntable. This comes with different-sized tripods.

A Ken Moore adjustable branch-bender for large branches.

Ken Moore and Gadgets4bonsai

Many people dream about turning their hobby into a business and livelihood; for one such person, this ambition has come true. Ken Moore is a committed bonsai enthusiast and has been a member of the Northamptonshire Bonsai Society (UK), or NBS, since 1999. He has twenty-five trees in different stages of training. Through the Northamptonshire Bonsai Society, he was fortunate to meet Paul Goff, an experienced and talented member for many years, who has written and photographed a superb piece on the tokonoma (see page 223). Through Paul, Ken acquired some show-quality trees, including a group planting of larch that was once featured on the front of a bonsai magazine.

Ken became involved in making bonsai tools when Paul Goff asked him to apply his welding and design skills to building a lifting device for moving Paul's large, plastic, tree containers. Paul had struggled for years when moving his containers, often having to ask strong friends around just to move a tree. Ken designed a stretcher system that could lift containers weighing over 220 pounds (100 kg).

A favorite tool for many folk who like big trees is the Ken Moore branch-bender. This is a fearsome tool that is designed to make heavy bends in branches and trunks up to 2½ inches (6 cm) thick. As the tool is fully adjustable, thick branches can be bound with raffia, wired and then bent with precision. The branch-bender has recently been tested by Farrand Bloch, editor of *Bonsai Europe* magazine, on a juniper, with excellent results. I received mine recently and managed to bend branches up to 2 to 3 inches (5–7 cm) without breaking them, or my hand. The tool has good balance and looks good, too.

Ken's wonderful turntable is a joy to use, and the best that I have seen. It has two interchangeable sets of legs so that the table can be used in different situations and at differing heights. The oil-finished, wooden turntable has a bearing system for smooth movement and is lockable.

Arbortech woodworking tools

The Australian company Arbortech has spread around the world. I started using its woodcarving, circular discs over fifteen years ago, when the first Arbortech tool came out in the UK. I have seen it develop a number of excellent tools since then. The extension arm for the angle-grinder allows small cutters to be attached. The new industrial grade of saw is excellent on angle-grinders, and I love the new power chisels.

The Arbortech Pro cutting blade and replaceable cutters.

An angle-cutter by Arbortech.

Flex Cut

I was introduced to a great toy when demonstrating at the MidAtlantic Bonsai Societies event in New Jersey recently. It is the Swiss Army knife of hand chisels, and folds up into a spring-loaded system. I now use this when I need to carry out some detailed refinement on my own trees and do not want to carry a huge kit around. It's fast, instant and very sharp. It is made by Flex Cut, and you can purchase it through Jim Doyle in America.

The Arbortech extension arm for detail-carving.

The Arbortech power chisel allows detailed carving.

From Jim Doyle, USA, Flex Cut's Swiss Army knife–style carving tool, which has locking blades.

61

First styling of a yamadori Scots pine

Craig Coussins

This tree had never been styled. It was a kind of yamadori as it had escaped from a forestry development and had been growing in a bog. I had spent three years building its foliage, and now Rob Atkinson was going to help me to get it sorted.

It was quite an easy tree to style, but the preparation took all day. Old needles had to be cut off; I never pull these off as doing so causes a lot of damage and attracts aphids. Cut the needles just above the sheath, and the sheath falls off after drying up naturally.

The wiring to the tips meant that we could create the foliage pads by bending the thin and straggly growth into shape (see the Belgian Scots pine on page 136).

After removing the main crossing root (there is another, but that will be sorted out next year), Rob and I went to work on the dead branch halfway up the trunk that had split slightly away from the main trunk. The result is pleasing and will look great next year, when the growth fills out. The determined front had a badly crossing root, which was removed. The broken jinned area was not essential, and a design decision to remove it was made. The same jin was later incorporated into another pine with an inverse taper. The shari was then extended into the area from which the jin was removed. The flowers developing into seed cones were removed. The two-year-old needles, or old, back needles, were removed. Extensive wiring was now required to place the branches, starting from the bottom, in order to open up the space.

The other images in this section are of inspirational pines that I found around Scotland.

This tree has not been styled yet.

The ugly crossing root.

The healthy root was cut.

The root was pulled back.

Be careful when cutting.

We then needed to shape the area for a uro hole. This will later heal naturally.

Applying cut paste with moist fingers enables it to stay on the tree, not your hands.

Cut paste keeps a wound moist until the cambium rolls over.

Applying small bits of bark disguises the cut area until it heals.

The area has now been covered.

Removing two-year-old needles allows new buds to grow.

The growth was developed for three years.

Now the dense growth needs to be thinned out.

Only cut old needles, taking care not to damage the branch.

Cut the needles, and they will fall off without "weeping."

Always work at the correct height, with your back straight.

The needles are now cleaned and are easier to shape.

Bending long, thin twigs into the pad. Don't bend a twig twice in case you fracture it.

Bending long, thin twigs into a foliage pad.

Start from the base of the tree and work upward.

The left side after wiring and shaping.

The back of the tree.

I pulled the jin down the trunk to make a natural shari.

The front of the tree. Note the large jin halfway up.

The jin was partly broken.

This reveals a natural image of dead wood (shari).

Visible healing told me that the jin had already broken.

The edges were sealed with cut paste, letting the cambium roll over.

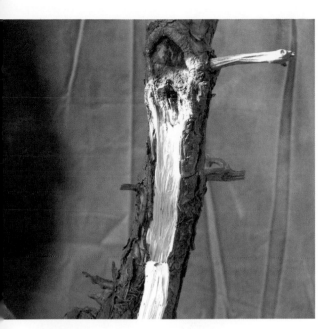

The first styling. This will take another three years to develop fully.

Craig and Rob with their day's work.

A windswept pine clump (Devon, UK).

An elegantly shaped pine (Carlisle, UK).

A dense Caledonian Scots pine (*Pinus sylvestris*).

What to do with the foliage
— remove, retain or reduce?

When first making a bonsai, you need to decide whether to keep branches or remove them in the first styling. On a healthy tree you can, of course, remove some branches. If a tree is less than 100 percent healthy, but is healthy enough for a styling, you may have to leave a branch to promote the tree's overall vigor. Remove that branch later, when the tree has fully recovered. Do not wire the branch that you intend to remove, other than simple guying to hold it away from the other branches. You can reduce the length of a long branch by zigzagging it slightly or massively to bring in the length. It is important to mist it while you are doing this to keep the leaves or needles moist and to prevent the branch from drying out. It is best not to repot and style in the same season as that could be stressful for the bonsai.

Maintaining the health of a tree
feeding and watering for each stage of the development or styling

It is normal to feed after a few weeks when repotting. Feeding may damage the new feeder roots. If you are just styling, it is better to wait for around two weeks for the tree to settle. It is probably all right to feed right away, but I am a little careful in this respect. Heavy feeding will push the tree to grow faster and put out more buds, but when that happens, you need to be aware of the growth. Remove the wire after a few weeks if it starts biting into the wood.

Ramification
the development of the fine twig structure to create foliage pads

For pines and maples, see pages 51 and 181.

- Never prune larch (*Larix*) during the growing season. Only prune back in the dormant, winter season, a month or so prior to bud-break. Prune back to the first set of new buds on that season's growth. If you cut back in summer, you will lose important new growth. *Larix* are best appreciated in winter; early spring, when new buds break like small, green stars; and fall, when the tree turns yellow.
- Most deciduous trees need the new growth at the ends of the branches pinching out throughout the growing season.
- Do not let such flowering plants as satsuki come into flower. Remove flower buds early on to direct the tree's energy to leaf growth instead.

Refinement
the removal, replacement or reshaping of existing material

In some cases, the removal, or jinning, of a branch is necessary for the developing image. I remember one of my trees, which was developing successfully until I left it in a nursery for a couple of years. While I was away, it was infected with vine weevil — a root-eating grub. By the time that the pest was identified, the tree was seriously weakened, and two of the branches had been lost. This required a substantial restyle that could only be done after repotting, cleaning out the soil and letting the tree regain its vigor for a couple of years. So be vigilant and keep an eye on the health of your tree.

First styling of *Juniperus procumbans*

Craig Coussins

Here are some examples of garden-center material and different ideas for creating something from them. *Juniperus procumbans* is ideal for this job. You can see what I did with them here.

First styling of *Juniperus procumbans*: before, 12 inches (30 cm).

First styling of *Juniperus procumbans*: after, 11 inches (28 cm).

First styling of *Juniperus procumbans*: before, 8 inches (20 cm).

First styling of *Juniperus procumbans*: after, 8 inches (20 cm).

First styling of *Juniperus procumbans*: before, 4 inches (10 cm).

First styling of *Juniperus procumbans*: after, 3 inches (8cm).

Rob Atkinson (UK) designs a garden juniper

This juniper — *Juniperus chinensis* "Old Gold" — was one of a batch that was dug up from an old shopping center. Rob trimmed back the foliage in year one and kept the tree for two years before setting to work. Using an angle-grinder with an Arbortech blade, he shaped the shari. He then fine-wired all of the foliage and separated the apex from the structure. All of the shape is from the top. The styling took Rob three hours.

Juniperus chinensis "Old Gold."

Wood dust is a carcinogen, so it is vital to wear a face mask.

Carving a natural shape.

Reducing overly large jins.

Wiring the tree.

The cut is sealed with Kiyonal to keep it moist.

The right side.

The right side.

The back.

The front.

The *Taxus* before work started.

Alternative front 1.

Alternative front 2.

The development of the image in the first years

First styling — groups

Designing a *Celtis* forest

Rob Clausen, South Africa

I met Rob in the early 1990s, when I was making a month-long tour of South Africa. I was teaching at some of the clubs and at the African Bonsai Convention in Johannesburg. Since then, this bonsai master has become one of the most outstanding artists in Africa, with a penchant for larger-sized bonsai. His lovely wife Sarah, herself an excellent bonsai teacher and artist, helps Rob with the care of his collection, which numbers in excess of a thousand trees. His knowledge and expertise in collecting and developing native material is second to none, and I have great respect for this fine designer.

I asked Rob to show two distinct examples of his work. Here, he looks at the initial preparation and development of a forest group. Later (see page 72) he discusses perspective in the planting.

White stinkwood (*Celtis africana*) and Chinese hackberry (*Celtis sinensis*)

The trees came from nursery stock, including the main tree, with some of the smaller trees already styled as bonsai. The oldest was field-grown for fifteen years in the ground. It was then potted and grown on for bonsai for four more years.

Feeding regime: None.
Soil: Composted mix with sand for free-draining.
Preparation: Carving was done at the time of lifting. The root ball was cut flat to the visible nebari and sealed using Kiyonal.
Maintenance: Planted into a growing pot to develop ramification. As there were no branches on the large tree, all branches were grown from the bare stump.
Next stage: Planted into a bonsai pot four years later to define the roots and begin the styling of the overall image.

These are the main points.
- Work with the trees to determine their initial placement in the group. The large tree in this image was discarded in favor of another, better-defined tree.
- Leaving the trees in their pots until you are ready to do the actual placement reduces the stress on them. All of the trees used here had been in pots for a minimum of a year, and some for longer.
- In the five years after this session, a number of changes were made. Some small trees at the back and center of the planting were removed from the group as they disrupted the visual speed of the image. To create a negative area within the group (a clear area that forms part of the overall image, and so part of the design), I needed to reduce the number of trees as the design was overcrowded. The major tree comes into leaf a few weeks after the other, younger trees. Now you can see the clarity of the design and how the image flows (the visual speed) without disruption from the nonessential elements of the design.
- The final image is remarkably like the original sketch.
- Planned design changes for the future may reflect this digitally altered image.

Planning the *Celtis* forest.

There is no drama in this image.

This is a good perspective.

The *Celtis* forest group makes a group in 1996!

Celtis forest: the drawing made in 1996.

The *Celtis* forest, Christmas 1997.

The *Celtis* forest in 2004. The completed arrangement.

The *Celtis* forest, spring 2003. The apex showed some
damage, which was repaired one year later.

Celtis group on rock — Rob Clausen

The trees: Prior to placing them in a bonsai growing bed, I cut the major roots, sealed them with Kiyonal and removed a major root at the back and above the nebari (surface root) structure. All cuts above the ground were sealed with a mix of 20 percent Kiyonal and 80 percent PVA wood glue.

The cuts were resealed during the subsequent growing period to avoid dehydration of the cambium and promote better healing of the edge of the cambium growth. This technique is necessary because some woods will rot at large cuts. Species such as maple (*Acer*) and hackberry (*Celtis*) are particularly susceptible to rotting in large cut areas, and when rot occurs, the bark may not roll over. It is therefore important to seal the large cut surface immediately, thereby reducing the risk of die-back and subsequent growth damage to the bonsai.

The rock: This was originally collected by the late Werner Bub in South Africa. Werner gave it to me a number of years ago. The rock was very heavy, and for this demonstration I needed three identical pots that were quite different to conventional bonsai pots in that I wanted to emulate an almost floating image. The rocks needed to be lighter visually as well as actually. The curved base would allow me to achieve this. I needed three pots to demonstrate perspective planting and the illusion of distance and size. The first pot was planted with a small tree and a large expanse of sand and moss. This gave the illusion of size, both in the tree and in the landscape. The second was a closer view, where the trees occupied more space within the landscape. The final pot was a close-up view, with a large tree in the foreground and smaller trees in the background, giving a large tree image and the perspective of depth.

- To create the duplicate rocks, I selected the split line on the rock.
- I applied a wax coating (floor polish), which acted as a barrier and release agent to the following stage.
- I covered the working surface with latex mixed with wood flour (very fine sawdust). This prevented the latex from shrinking and therefore provided the body that I required.
- I applied fifteen coats of the mix, adding each one as the previous coat dried.
- The latex was left in place at this stage.
- Over the top of the latex, I laid three layers of fiberglass resin and fiberglass matting, which were left in place.
- I built a wooden frame to fit the contors of the fiberglass, and then glued that to the surface, using more fiberglass resin.
- The frame supported the fiberglass mold, which would otherwise have been flexible.
- The fiberglass shell, now dry, was lifted off the latex coating and the latex coating was carefully peeled from the original rock.
- The fiberglass mould was turned upside down and the latex mold, which fitted exactly to the fiberglass shell, was fully supported.
- A mix of sculpting cement and binders was laid down into the negative mold. I used polypropylene cloth in this mix to enable me to build depth. I layered the mix five times — mix, cloth, mix and so on.
- The bottom of the rock was hand-sculpted to give the natural shape and texture that I needed.
- The rock was watered over a period of five days to allow slow hardening and eventual strength.
- When the rock was dry, I turned it over and removed the negative fiberglass and latex mold so that I could repeat the process to make two more identical rocks.
- Two weeks later, I painted the rocks with a clear PVA coating, which provided a natural finish while acting as a barrier between the rock and the plant roots.
- The final image of 11 months later shows the clarity of the group in balance with the rock. A great lightness was achieved through the concave shape, which in itself balances on a small point.

Celtis group, pot A.

Celtis group, pot B.

Adding reinforced layers.

Wood is cut to fit the shape.

Paint latex on top. The new, "copy" pot.

That's now reinforced with a wooden frame.

A layer of screed and polypropylene is added.

The main trunk is planted out and left to grow.

The *Celtis* group undergoes constant pruning over two years.

The main tree now displays good ramification and strong growth.

The heavy trunk cut is rolling over.

The heavy roots that were split and sealed.

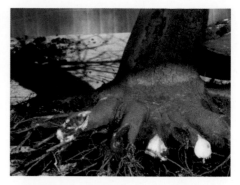

The long roots from the first planting were reduced.

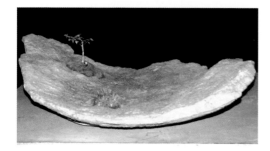

Demonstrating perspective.

The second group, with smaller trees positioned at the back.

A close-up view of the second group.

The final planting in the series.

The rear: a far view.

The planting 11 months later, showing refinement.

Maintenance

After the design

The overall maintenance of any bonsai is a continuing process of pruning, styling, wiring, unwiring, and feeding.

- The wiring and unwiring takes time and will need to be done on a regular basis. Over a period of ten years, you may have to do this between ten and fifteen times.
- Pinching and pruning to develop the ramification, shape and density of the tree needs to be done throughout the growing period.

In other words, it is as much work to maintain a bonsai as it is to make one. A tree will soon grow out of its final shape if pinching and pruning is not kept up. The fine, developing roots will continue to grow, albeit slowly if the upper portion of the bonsai is kept pruned. However, the roots will grow very fast if the upper portion is left to grow without pruning the leaves and lengthening shoots.

Buying a "finished" bonsai

Unless you understand the techniques needed for maintenance, it may be better to buy a finished bonsai or penjing. Otherwise, you will inevitably end up with a bush or a tree that has too many roots through the upper-portion growth.

Buying a finished bonsai is to accept that it depends on your ability to care for it. In Japan and some European countries, masterpiece trees are cared for by specialist growers or nurseries. The owner leaves the tree in their care and only sees it when he or she requires the tree for display. Some people have the money to build a collection of other people's bonsai artworks. While they may not be fully conversant with all of the techniques required to maintain a collection of fine bonsai, they will be able to employ someone who does. However, they should understand that the pinching and control of foliage pads is almost a full-time occupation when you have a collection. I have to pinch and prune some of the trees in my collection, especially the elms and zelkovas, at least once or twice a month. In some countries, that job needs to be done twice a week.

Pinching — development of the foliage pads

In maintaining a bonsai, you will need to prune back, on a regular basis, the growing shoots. Pines (*Pinus*) are an exception as they will grow more slowly than junipers (*Juniperus*) or elms (*Ulmus*). I use scissors to trim back to the shape or to allow growth to the shape that I would like. My own teacher, thirty years ago, referred to this part of maintenance as hedge-pruning or topiary. Well it's not that, of course, but you will find that it has similarities. Always use a sharp knife, and seal any cut larger than a young, soft shoot or die-back will result.

Placement of branches — for design and health

If a branch is struggling because, usually, it is low down on the trunk and is, by default, a weaker branch, it will need maintenance. If the branch is necessary, it is best not to pinch it until it has regained its vigor. You may also have to consider moving the branch into a lighter area. Making sure that the tree is regularly turned to receive even light will also ensure a good growth balance around the branches.

Problems-solved checklist

You may find the following checklist useful.

- *Branches too long:* Reduce the length through wiring. When wiring to reduce length, protect the branch by wrapping raffia or vet wrap around it. Always bend where there will be a bud on the outside of the bend. In larger branches, it is sometimes best to carry out extreme bending over a period of two years. Some species, such as junipers, will need constant misting while you are bending.

- *A branch too short:* In some species, the natural form is to grow comparatively short branches. Sequoias have short branches in comparison to their overall size, as do kauri and some pines. A solution may be to make all of the branches short and so establish an image that is balanced. In a case where length is required, allowing a branch to grow is a long process, unless you feed well. To thicken the branch, remove the tip to allow side shoots to form.

- *Aging:* This will depend on the tree's overall appearance and the characteristics of the image. Overall appearance includes the length of the branches. If they are too long, the tree can look too young. Reducing the length will give a more mature look to the bonsai. Carving or creating a shari or uro (hole) will also imply age.

- *Bonsai on rocks:* Attach trees to awkward areas with peat muck, a mix of clay and peat or organic compost. Use the peat muck to build a low wall around the area that you wish to plant in order to retain soil.

- *Up or down branching:* Placement of branches is important, and the catch-all bending-down of a branch is not always the right solution when wiring a bonsai. Not many species of trees have downward-growing branches, and most pines have upward-branching ones. Cedars', generally, grow downward. Consider wiring a long branch upwards and dropping the foliage pad. Older trees may have a slightly downward-pointing branch placement, but wiring every tree using that method shows a lack of understanding of how a tree grows in nature. There is also the risk that every tree that you design looks the same.

- *Bud placement:* Wire to the tip of every bud and elevate the buds to form the pad. Leaving a bud in a straight or downward-pointing shape will cause the tree to grow to length. Elevating the tip stops the length from developing at that point and helps to form a good foliage pad.

First styling: *Acer palmatum*

Craig Coussins

In this demo, I look at the first styling of an old, cut-down maple (*Acer palmatum*). A few years ago, I had to clear out some land with mature trees on it, including a number of full-sized, forty-year-old *Acer palmatum*. I lifted all of them after removing all of the upper foliage and sealing the large cuts. Not one died. The feeder roots are easy to develop on maples, so I also cut right back to the nebari. This little tree was left over from that time, and I decided that it now needed to be styled. All of the branches and fine twigs were created from the trunk over a period of ten years. I had just never got round to making it into a bonsai.

Before leaf removal in summer.

The front.

The left side.

The right side.

The back after leaf removal.

This has opened up the tree ready for wiring.

The front.

Trevor now cuts out any dead tips and twigs.

The new front.

The left side.

The new front. Foliage pads will soon develop.

The new back.

The right side.

Discovering satsuki azaleas

Kaho x

Gyoten

Nikko

Introduction by Craig Coussins

Rhododendrons and azaleas are found in North America, Japan and Southeast Asia. The tropical branch of the genus extends the range to New Guinea, and there is even one that is native to the tropical rainforests of northern Australia.

Rhododendrons and azaleas are very similar, and both belong to the family Ericaceae, in the genus *Rhododendron*. Most of the commonly cultivated rhododendrons are hybrids that have been produced by crossing different species. The species can be either evergreen or deciduous, and have either small or large leaves.

Azalea varieties are also hybrids, produced, in the main, from four rhododendron species. Generally, azaleas are classified into three groups, as follows.
- Mollis azaleas — these are deciduous types and grow well in cool conditions.
- Indica azaleas — these have larger and flashier flowers.
- Kurume azaleas — these have smaller flowers, but flower growth is normally denser on the tree.

Warm climates

Tropical rhododendrons are classified as vireyas. Most of them are relatively small, some being less than 3 feet tall (1 m), others perhaps growing to 6 feet (2 m). If you live in the subtropics, you can grow vireyas and indica azaleas.

Temperate climates

If you live in a temperate climate, you can grow mollis, indica and kurume azaleas.

Satsuki azaleas

In Japan, they started working with the hybridization of azaleas in the 15th century. The first book on azaleas appeared in Japan in 1661. By 1700, growers had a good understanding of azalea and rhododendron hybridization, and they had described over 160 varieties. Satsuki means "fifth month," which is when the satsuki azalea flowers. Today, there are 1,106 registered and officially recognized varieties of satsuki azaleas in Japan. (Some of the ones featured here are from the Gingko Collection in Belgium.)

Arthur Robinson is one of Australia's outstanding growers of satsukis, and has started teaching in many parts of this vast continent. He is also a world-class violin maker, and his attention to detail is second to none. I asked Arthur to share some of his enthusiasm for these lovely plants.

Satsukis

The flowering azaleas of Japan, by Arthur Robinson, Western Australia

These glorious plants flower later than the normal indica or kurume azaleas: in the northern hemisphere, from late May through June — satsuki means "fifth month" of the lunar calendar — and in the southern hemisphere, in around November and December.

When not in flower, they make magnificent bonsai. The nebari (surface roots) develop quickly and easily, and in fall, many varieties display strong oranges and reds in the leaves.

Issho no Haru

The satsuki species of azalea is *Rhododendron indicum,* but it has developed quite independently in Japan and usually has five or ten stamens. It mutates quite easily, hence the differing patterns of flowers on the same plant. Although some 1,500 to 2,000 varieties are listed, there are also many others that are unlisted.

Rhododendron tamurae (known in Japan as "maruba") is found in the warmer areas of Japan. When crossed with the colder-climate strains, it produces satsuki that can stand up well to heat. I have one called Fuji Mori that grows furiously during our hot summers.

Yama no Hikari

Some of the varieties are more suited to bonsai culture than others. This is partly to do with their flowers, but, more importantly, with their growth habit. Much is taken into consideration: small leaves, strong growth, quick development of good nebari, and flexibility for good wiring and shaping.

Cuttings

If a material tree is not available, then a nice tree can be started from a cutting. Once established, all low-growing buds and soft shoots are rubbed off, allowing one main shoot to grow. Later in the season, some curves can be put into it by wiring. Keep in mind that this will be the future trunk and will be much thicker. Subsequently, this cutting can be put into the ground, a wooden box, or a large pot to grow and develop, always removing basal shoots. In this way, a clean trunk can be developed free of ugly scars. I have seen beautiful seven- to ten-year-old bonsai displayed in Japan, so it need not take all that long to develop something good. The best time to take cuttings is around and after flowering time. Take off the new shoots using a downward tearing motion, leaving the heel untrimmed and removing all but four or five leaves. Stand the cuttings in water for half an hour and then put them into propagating sand. I use a cloche to maintain humidity levels — usually half of a plastic bottle on the pot. Alternatively, a seedling flat and a greenhouse can be used.

Kozan

Shuho no Hikari

Shinyo no Tsuki

Sachi no Hana

Gyoten Satsukis from Gingko
Nursery

Soil

The Japanese growers use Kanuma soil, often mixed with sphagnum moss, for their satsukis, and if available, this is a good way to go. Because I live in a Mediterranean climate, and Kanuma is unavailable in Australia (although that may soon change), I use two parts weathered pine-bark fines and one part gravel or sharp sand with trace elements. I find that this works very well, always bearing in mind that satsuki are acid-loving plants.

Styles

Satsukis can be grown in any style, but because their dead wood does not last like juniper wood, there are not many driftwood styles evident. In warmer climates, the semi- and full cascade are very popular as the pots for these are deep and retain moisture well.

Watering

These beautiful plants like plenty of water and excellent drainage and hate having wet feet. They will grow happily with a little fertilizer, which can be applied from spring to fall, with a pause while they flower.

Wiring

Yes, they are a little brittle, but wiring the new growth is a breeze. The bark is thin, so care must be taken, which provides excellent wiring practice! In spring, just before flowering and the accompanying spurt of growth, the small twigs are prone to coming away, so care must be taken at this time if you are removing or replacing wiring.

Problems

The greatest enemy is root rot, which can be controlled with a little preventative spraying using a suitable product in both winter and spring. At repotting time, it is a good idea to scrub the trunk and major branches with a toothbrush and water. Moss should only be present when the tree is displayed, and should not be growing up the trunk. Trunk- and branch-scrubbing results in a lot freer budding out and is hugely beneficial to the plant.

Transplanting

When repotting, I find that it is best to remove all of the very fine roots and to get back to more or less "fine twiggy" growth. This seems to lessen the chances of root rot, certainly where I live. Cut the roots back directly under the tree so that you form a mound shape, and arrange the soil accordingly. With very young material, be careful not to take off too many roots; you can leave some of the fine ones. With freshly rooted cuttings, the roots are all fine, so just rearrange these, keeping the future nebari in mind. You must cut away roots that are crossing over others to ensure good nebari.

The time for repotting varies according to the climate, but in Japan it is done just after flowering. Here, in Western Australia, I repot before flowering and remove the flower buds by pinching them off sideways.

Pruning

Satsukis are basal-shooting, and the top is weaker than that of most other trees. Satsuki tops are not thinned out heavily, but are wired into position to maintain a good balance. Too much pruning of the tree can weaken it considerably, so three to five branches, emanating from the same point and skillfully wired to shape, can often be seen in the top of a well-developed bonsai. Sometimes this will mean that the lower branches need heavier pruning to maintain balance. When about 75 percent of the flowers have come out, it is time to start thinking about removing all old and remaining flowers, as the setting of seed pods will weaken the tree considerably. Unless you are going to breed satsuki, simply pinch or cut them off with fine scissors. It is vitally important to make sure that you get all of the seed pods off the tree.

Himalayan Azalea Cutting collected Nepal 1965

De-budding

Flowering puts a strain on the plant, so to gain vegetative growth, which is essential during the developmental stage, it is necessary to remove the flower buds as they appear. They are quite distinctive, being little, hard, solid-looking, cone-shaped growths in the very center of the shoot. The easiest way to remove them is to push them to the left or right, while maintaining a hold on the twig, and then they come away quite easily. You can also use scissors if you prefer. It is desirable to balance the number of flowers on a tree that you are going to allow to flower. Where they are too crowded, simply pinch them off. It is always tempting to want to enjoy the flowers. I rotate my flowering so that I have some sort of display each year.

Himalayan Azalea flower intense fuschia pink comes in 6th month

Recommended varieties

Some varieties that work well in bonsai culture are: kinsai, osakazuki, chinsan, gyoten, issho-no-haru, kaho, yama-no-hikari, suzu-no-homare, hinotsukasa, hakatajiro, takasago, izayoi, juko, yata no kagami, shinkyo, matsu kagami, matsunami, and their related varieties. In cold climates, kozan, nikko, nyohozan, hakurei, korin, sachi-no-hana and other relatives are also successful.

Hybridization by bees

Aftercare

Here are some notes for the aftercare of more mature satsukis. This is not a full care list for satsukis, but a guideline for seasonal care and maintenance.

1. *Early spring:* This is the time for repotting young trees and after flowering for more mature trees. Repotting in spring means that initially you can only trim the smaller shoots lightly. Wait until later spring, or warmer weather, to perform more structural pruning. Otherwise, wait until after flowering for heavier pruning.
2. *Watering:* Do not water the foliage of the tree when the flower buds start to form as that can induce disease and flower abortion.
3. *Weak growth:* If the tree is slightly weak, or needs more leaves, remove all of the flower buds that year to direct the vigor of the growing period to creating new leaves instead of flowers.
4. *Pruning:* Prune out flower buds after flowering. Remove all of the flower structure as soon as the flower starts wilting. Remove the shell, stamen and so on until you are left with nothing. This stops the flower from going to seed and therefore reducing the vigor of the tree for next year.

Insect pollination originally caused varieties

Kunio Kobayashi created this outstanding satsuki azalea, which he calls *Kika Ku* **("The Tortoise and Crane"). The name means "to live very long" as, according to Japanese mythology, the crane and tortoise are thought to live for to over a thousand years.**

A satsuki azalea created by the prize-winning and outstanding bonsai master Kunio Kobayashi.

5. *Light trimming:* Trim out the leaves after flowering. Cut the leaves in half to encourage new buds to form on the shoot. The nutrition of the satsuki needs to be balanced, and leaving all of the leaves on will cause the tree to grow to length instead of density. This is an opportunity to style or restyle the satsuki. When trimming the shoots on satsukis, cut the new shoot in half and new buds will form within a month. Alternatively, when the satsuki flowers are forming, the plant puts out several shoots behind the flower bud — usually five. Tear these off backward, leaving two shoots, which can be cut back to two leaves, thus developing a good 2 x 2 structure.

6. *Watering:* Water in the morning and in the afternoon if you have warm days. Satsukis like a lot of water during the growing period, but do not like the pot sitting in water. Root rot is then possible. Protect satsukis from rains when the flower buds are forming. Keep them under cover. Tilt the pots to drain off excess water.

7. *Potting:* Use Kanuma on its own, and do not mix it with other soils. Lifting any azalea from the ground and mixing the existing soil with Kanuma may lead to root rot, so remove all soil from the plant first and repot it in pure Kanuma. All azaleas and rhododendrons require cool, moist, acid soil with a pH of 4.5 to 5.5. Before Kanuma was available in the West, we tended to use peat as our soil base. That had the problem, in bonsai culture, of either retaining too much water or drying out too quickly and then not having the ability to reconstitute. We used to mix peat with grit or sharp sand, and while we managed to produce reasonable plants, we never had real control of the soil, and for many it was a hit-or-miss scenario. If you are cautious by nature, you can repot by cutting pie-shaped wedges out of the root ball and then slowly replacing the soil and roots over a few years.

8. *Feeding:* Balanced liquid fertilizers — Miracle-Gro, for example — used weekly, will induce leaf growth. When the required leaf development has been achieved, use potassium-rich materials, such as tomato fertilizer, to promote flowers. There are fertilizer blocks, or "cakes," such as Bio Gold, that are used in bonsai culture and that are suitable for satsukis. These can be spread around the soil surface from early spring, when growth has started, to a month prior to flowering. They can be reapplied to the soil after flowering. After flowering, wait at least 10 to 14 days before starting to refertilize. After this period, apply a half-strength liquid fertilizer to the soil. Increase this after a further 10 days to two-thirds strength, and then a month later to blocks. Applying too much fertilizer after flowering can inhibit the development of the new buds for next year. The tree is a little weak after flowering, so you must apply fertilizer slowly and gradually after that period. Special azalea fertilizers can be found at most garden stores. Over-fertilizing can cause a lot of damage to plants. The signs of over-fertilization include sudden leaf-drop and brown leaf tips. To prevent this type of damage, apply light feedings in early spring to induce leafing, and then tomato fertilizer after flowering to help the development of the flower buds, which will form by midsummer to early fall. Stop fertilizing at least a month prior to flowering. Remove any soil-surface fertilizer blocks.

9. *Summer:* Reduce feeding in midsummer when the weather is very hot as most trees enter a semi-dormancy period, which is caused by excessive heat. Keep your satsukis out of bright, direct sunshine as they prefer slight shade.

10. *Fall:* The satsuki will have completed its growth by now, so stop feeding and be careful about watering. Keep the soil watered, but be aware of colder days arriving in temperate climates. Satsukis, like other trees, do not feed during the winter and dormant periods.

A basic large tree repot

Although smaller trees are relatively easy to repot, larger trees, such as satsukis, can be a problem. Firstly, you really need a friend to help you. Secondly, you must prepare all of the soil and materials that you will need. This European beech (*Fagus sylvatica*) was in need of a repot, having been in this pot for three years. Three months after the work, excellent growth meant that the tree needed a good prune to stay in shape. My old teacher used to say that repotting a tree sometimes means that the tree does not know what hit it. It can respond by growing a bit faster than you would have liked.

Use the mix recommended for the particular species.

Sieve out the fines. The soil must be free-draining, and that means no fine, tiny material.

The fines will compact the soil. Do not use the fines as top dressing as that would compact.

You are left with the right size of dust-free soil particles, in this case, of Akadama.

Examine the soil.

Carefully look for root aphids, which are identified as small, blue-white ovals.

Use a root hook to tease out the old soil and root mass.

If you cut large roots, be sure to seal the cuts with Kiyonal or a suitable latex.

Use a sharp "pull" saw to remove thick root-mass areas on the outside.

Check that the roots will fit into the new pot.

Place your soil mix in the pot, mounding it up to allow easier penetration of the root ball.

Three months later, a healthy tree with new soil will reward you with a lot of new growth.

Aftercare and development of bonsai

A satsuki azalea created by the prize-winning and outstanding bonsai master Kunio Kobayashi.

Spring buds on one of my large _Larix_ groups: back view.

While understanding that we need to water, feed and repot from time to time, the most important aspect of bonsai and penjing care is maintenance, or ongoing aftercare.

- Wiring and unwiring is a regular event. In most species, it is required once a year, but in warmer countries, and with different and fast-growing species, it may need to be done twice.
- Checking wires to ensure that none of them are biting into the structure is an ongoing and daily task.
- Cutting the wire off, stage by stage, is always necessary — usually from the strongest parts first, such as the apex and the tips of the branches.
- A regime of correct feeding will need to be in place to make sure that the tree remains healthy.
- Checking for insects is an ongoing and daily part of a cycle that will include a soil-drench to combat sub-surface pests.
- Turning the tree around to make sure that equal growth takes place is required every week.
- Removing moss from the lower trunk area and nebari (surface roots) to avert dampness on the bark and prevent insects from being harboured in that area is necessary.
- Weed removal is also a weekly chore. This increases the amount of food available to the tree rather than to the weeds.
- Placement is required throughout the year to gain light or to reduce light on midsummer days, when the trees may need some shade.
- Constant pruning of tops, unless you are growing a bonsai into a shape, is necessary. Tip-pruning is required to encourage new twigs and so increase ramification, or twig structure development.
- Taking photographs twice a year, in leaf and out of leaf, if it is a deciduous tree, is advisable. This will enable you to see the development of the tree.
- Protection is required in cooler climates over winter, or throughout the year at high elevations, where frost can hit any time of the year.

盆栽

chapter 3
bonsai styles
and collections

There are many styles of bonsai, and this section looks at them in detail. Natural trees are shown in their landscape setting and then, where possible, these images are replicated in the book. In this chapter, we also take a look at collections of bonsai and penjing from around the globe, where different styles evolve.

Styles of bonsai

Beech (*Fagus sylvatica*) cascade. (V Gianotti CC.)

Informal upright *Pinus nigra*. (V Gianotti CC.)

Literati *Pinus nigra*. (V Gianotti CC.)

A three-thousand-year-old giant kauri in New Zealand.

Informal upright *Pinus nigra*. (V Gianotti CC.)

Informal upright *Pinus sylvestrus*. (V Gianotti CC.)

Literati *Pinus sylvestrus*. (V Gianotti CC.)

***Cupressus macrocarpa* (Monterey cypress), raft style (Australia).**

There are many styles of bonsai, and all refer to styles in nature. Many have Japanese names, such as ikadabuki, netsuranari, nebari, and shari. Although these terms originated in Japan, they have become generic and, like Latin names for garden plants, allow everyone, no matter what country he or she is in, to understand one another. In China, where the other great art of penjing (the Chinese name for bonsai) originated, they have many styles reflecting the variety in the landscape. The five main regions of China each have a number of different forms.

My point is that we grow bonsai or penjing outside Japan or China, and so we have to work with our native trees to reflect the styles that we see around us in our own country's landscapes. This means that we should be taking the opportunity to create unique styles of American, Australian, African, or Scottish bonsai, and not just Japanese or Chinese styles.

John Yoshio Naka was a great American–Japanese teacher and authority on styles and size definitions. He identified the major styles and heights, which helps us to determine the style descriptions. John is no longer with us, but, like many others who studied with him over the years, I learned these styles from him, and have put his descriptions in the chart below. This is a good start to understanding the names in both Japanese and in English; Chinese styles have their own terminology. I teach in many different countries where English is not the prime language, so the terminology is useful as everyone will understand "chokkan" rather than "formal upright." I prefer using the English terminology in English-speaking countries, however. I have also listed the Japanese and English names of some of the most commonly used trees.

Japanese name	English name
Chokkan	Formal upright – no curves or bends in the trunk.
Moyogi	Informal upright – trunk changing direction.
Shakan	Slanted.
Sho-shakan	Small slant.
Chu-shakan	Medium slant.
Dai-shakan	Extreme slant.
Hankan	Very coiled trunk.
Fukinagashi	Windswept.
Bankan	Old, coiled trunk.
Saba kan	Hollow trunk.
Shari kan	Exposed dead wood on the trunk.
Shari miki	Dead wood, with dead branch stumps like fish bones.

Neijikan	Twisted-in-wind trunk and/or branches.
Kobukan	Lumpy trunk, gnarled with age.
Kengai	Cascade.
Han kengai	Semi-cascade.
Dai kengai	Straight cascade, extreme or long.
Gaito kengai ju shin	A tree with a round apex that is on the edge and cascades.
Taki kengai	A cascade changing direction.
Ito kengai	Multiple thin cascades.
Takan kengai	Twin, or more, trunks cascade.
Netsuranari	Raft style from roots.
Ikada	Raft style of trees from fallen trunk.
Ikadabuki	Raft style from a fallen tree, branches take root.
Soju	Twin trunks.
Sokan	Two trunks of differing sizea from a single root.
Yose-uye ("Yohsay-ooay")	Forest/group style.
Tako zukuri	Octopus style — very twisted branches and trunk.
Ishi-zuke	Root over rock.
Ne-agari	Exposed-root style — erosion-exposed roots.
Hoki dachi	Broom style — fan shape with even growth.
Bunjin literati	Similar to elegant sum-i paintings — long trunk, with slight growth at top, not heavy.

Windswept larch group. (Kevin Wilson School.)

Juniperus (juniper) cascade. (PO.)

Japanese tree name	English tree name
Momji or kaede	Maple.
Sugi	Japanese cedar.
Keyaki	Japanese gray-bark elm.
Ichijiku	Fig.
Shide or soro	Hornbeam.
Goyo-matsu (mats)	Five-needle white pine (*Pinus pentaphylla*).
Kuro-matsu (mats)	Japanese black pine, two-needles.
Shimpaku	Juniper (the most popular juniper grown as bonsai).
Kashu shimpaku	California juniper. Also Utah and other, similar species, such as western juniper and common juniper (*Juniperus communis*).
Benishitan	Cotoneaster.
Botangi	Buttonwood, silver buttonwood (from warmer climes in America, such as Florida).
Kashi, kunugi,	Oak — many varieties.
Maki podocarpus	Pine.
Satsuki	Flowering azalea.
Kurume	Azaleas.
Ezo-matsu	Japanese, jezo, ezo or yezo spruce.

Formal upright *Acer buerg*, or trident maple. (PO.)

Large broom style. (Australia.)

Literati itogawa *Juniperus* (juniper).

Informal upright *Juniperus* (juniper).

Literati pine. (PO.)

Root over rock maple (*Acer buergirianum*). (Gilbert van der Elst.)

Root over rock
Pyracantha. (PO.)

***Cryptomeria* group**
11¹/₂ feet (3.5 m).

Formal upright J.
Smith *Podocarpus*
(TZ-DM.)

Ichii	Japanese, American or English yew.
Sarusuberi	Crepe myrtle.
Tsuge	Box — stiff when old, but great for bonsai.

Other terms*	**English**
Ara-kawacho & arakawa	Rough bark.
Matsu (mats)	Pine.
Bonsai ju-shin	The top of a bonsai.
Shoki	Collected tree that is well established as a bonsai.
Yamadori*	Collected natural material for bonsai or natural bonsai not yet refined into a bonsai.
Tangei	Bonsai material or material good for making a bonsai.
Bonsai	A tree in a tray or container (from the Chinese *pentsai* — later Sung Dynasty).
Bonkei	Pentsai in China — landscapes with other plants, animals, figures, buildings and so on.
Bonseki, Bonsekei	Landscape planting, but no figures; only rocks, moss and trees.
Uro	Hole in a trunk with healed edges.
Nebari*	Surface roots.
Saba miki	Split trunk.
Shari kan	Bark split from trunk.
Shari* & sharimiki	Exposed areas on trunk. Dead trunk areas, with jinned twigs sticking out like spines.
Jin* or jinn*; jinning	Exposed areas on branches or tips. To remove bark and create dead wood.
Dai	Table on which to display a bonsai.
Daiza	Shaped table or a base for a suiseki.

* Common terms

Richard Poli, raft-style
privet (*Ligustrum*).
Australia.

Richard Poli, broom-
style *Ficus*. Australia.

Moyogi juniper with
shari and jin. (PO.)

Raft style in nature.

Acer buergirianum.

Windswept style.

Windswept literati
***Taxus* (yew).**

Juniper, styled by Craig Coussins,
developed over two years by Simon
Misdale, New Zealand.

Bonsai heights and names

Many years ago, John taught that we needed to have a structure of size descriptions as well. Bonsai come in a variety of heights, ranging from 1 inch (25 cm) to 6 feet (21 m). Essentially, the larger bonsai are known as garden bonsai or yard trees, while most bonsai are of a reasonable size, around a maximum of 40 inches (100 cm). In some quarters, a tree that requires two people to carry it is regarded simply as a big tree in a pot, and is not accepted as a true bonsai. However, there are no fixed criteria for bonsai, and this size chart is just a guide.

Sizes are measured from the soil level to the apex of the bonsai. The pot should enhance the tree and act as a frame to a picture. It should be seen, but not seen. A pot should not take over from the tree, but should have a quiet elegance in its own right. It should never be a distraction.

Styrax. **(ABBA–JOB. Association of British Bonsai Artists Convention–The Joy of Bonsai.)**

Height	Name	English or other name
1 inch (2.5 cm)	Keishi tsubo	Thimble size — within the shohin category.
1–3 inches (2.5–7.6 cm)	Shito	Mini size — very small — within the shohin category.
3–6 inches (7.6 – 15 cm)	Mame*	Mini size — within the shohin category.
6–8 inches (15 – 20 cm)	Shohin*	Katade — small size, also gafu-bonsai, or miyabi-bonsai (gafu is a term for excellent small-sized bonsai).
8–16 inches (20 – 40.6 cm)	Kifu-Sho or kifu	Small to medium size.
16–24 inches (40.6 – 61 cm)	Chu	Chuhin — medium size.
24–40 inches (61 – 101 cm)	Dai (also oomono)	Both terms mean large size, but oomono means a large size that can be carried by one man.
41–65 inches (104 – 165 cm)		Very large-sized bonsai — sometimes termed yard bonsai — that needs two men to carry it. Not always accepted as bonsai in competition (subjective).

*Most popular descriptions

Literati *Taxus*. (ABBA–JOB.)

Informal upright. (ABBA–JOB.)

Clump-style *Taxus*. (ABBA–JOB.)

Shimpaku juniper semi-cascade. (ABBA–JOB.)

White-pine moyogi. (*P. parv*–ABBA–JOB.)

White-pine semi-cascade. (ABBA–JOB.)

Juniperus squamata literati. (ABBA–JOB.)

Semi-cascade white pine. (ABBA–JOB.)

Semi-cascade white pine. (ABBA–JOB.)

Clump-style hornbeam. (ABBA–JOB.)

Semi-cascade European black pine. (I. Stewardson.)

Literati *Taxus*. (ABBA–JOB.)

Maple clump. (M. & R. Cooper.)

Maple clump. (M. & R. Cooper.)

Spruce literati. (J. P. Polman.)

Collections from around the world

Now we will look at some collections from around the world that contain a selection of trees in various sizes.

African bonsai

Flat-top bonsai

Photographed at the African Bonsai Association Convention in South Africa, by Duncan Wiles. On pages 148 to 149, Charles Ceronio, from South Africa, shows a flat-top-style group typical of the African veldt, while Rob Clausen illustrates African rock-style bonsai.

Charles Ceronio's white olive buddleia.

L. Nel, *Buddleja saligna*. (ABA–DW.)

T. Roos, *Olea europaea*, var. *africana*.

Charles Ceronio, *Acacia galpinii*. (ABA–DW.)

L. Nel, *Buddleja saligna*. (ABA–DW.)

W. Kotze, *Buddleja saligna*. (ABA–DW.)

J. Neethling, *Ligustrum obtusifolium* (small-leaf privet). (ABA–DW.)

L. Pieters, *Acacia burkei*. (ABA–DW.)

American bonsai

America has some incredible bonsai artists. These are some of their trees. (MABS stands for the Mid-Atlantic Bonsai Societies.)

George Le Bolt, of the U.S.A.

Juniperus chinensis, San Jose. (MABS.)

Thuja occidentalis. (MABS.)

Chinese elm (*Ulmus parvifolia*). (YiT 20 MABS 0.)

Shimpaku juniper 2. The Dugger Collection, Atlanta.

Box (*Buxus*). (10 YiT MABS 0.)

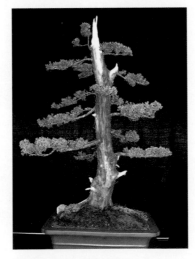

A thirty-year-old *Juniperus chinensis*. (1 YiT MABS.)

G. Le Bolt, variegated weeping fig (*Ficus benjamina variegata*).

Thuja occidentalis (Eastern white cedar). (MABS.)

George Le Bolt, Brazilian rain tree. (Sulochana Srinivasan 03.)

Chinese elm (*Ulmus parvifolia*). (YiT 20 MABS 0.)

Sawara cypress (*Cham. pisif.*). (YiT 20 MABS 0.)

Jim Smith

Jim is one of America's most respected masters. He specializes in figs and small-leaf jade trees. He shows some of his wonderful Florida collection here. Jim has also written a section on growing *Portulacaria afra* (see page 194).

Ficus salicifolia nerifolia.

Ficus salicifolia nerifolia.

Portulacaria. (JS.)

Ficus, Green Island 2. (JS.)

Ficus natalensis (Natal fig). (TZ–DM.)

Strangler fig.

Ficus salicifolia, 36 x 41 inches (91.4 x 104 cm) . (Jim TZ–DM.)

Bougainvillea. (JS.)

Sal rock.

Portulacaria afra. (J. Smith 020 TZ–DM.)

Ficus salicifolia (willow-leaf fig). (J. Smith 021 TZ-DM.)

Neea buxifolia.

Ficus nitida. (J. Smith 018.)

Ilex vomitoria nana. (J. Smith 017.)

Podocarpus. (TZ–DM.)

Ficus salicifolia nerifolia.
(J. Smith 019.)

Ficus retusa nitida (Cuban laurel).
(TZ–DM.)

Ficus, Green Island fig.

Ficus salicifolia nerifolia.

Ficus salicifolia nerifolia.

Tabebuia heterophylla.

Celtis sinensis (hackberry).

Ficus salicifolia nerifolia.

Fukien Tea, by Jim Smith.

Ficus retusa nitida.

Ficus salicifolia nerifolia.

Australian bonsai

I was both surprised and delighted by the quality of Aussie trees. The folk down under are extremely welcoming, hospitable, and willing to learn from their frequent visitors. Saying that, I saw some collections of such quality that the owners were obviously able to teach me a few things — and often did. In my opinion, they should be teaching much farther afield than Australia.

Many bonsai enthusiasts are troubled by theft. Many growers believe that most of these thefts are carried out by a particular group of people who sell the stolen trees within their own community. I suspect that the buyers are unaware of, or do not care to know, the source of the trees that they purchase. As a by-product, the thieves now sustain quite an industry — big dogs, barbed wire, trip alarms, and electrified fences are all the rage.

Craig Wilson and one of his banksias.

Craig Wilson, *Ficus retusa*.

Craig Wilson, *Banksia*.

Craig Wilson

Craig is a quiet man who runs a small, beautiful nursery in the mountains where he lives. His collection is not huge, but it is special. I saw some of the best banksia bonsai in Australia at his home. Like many Australian growers, Craig has been plagued by thefts, so his collection is best kept secret.

Craig Wilson, *Casuarina* (Australian pine).

Craig Wilson, *Banksia serrata* Old Man.

Craig Wilson, *Cedrus atlantica glauca.*

Craig Wilson, saw leak, or Old Man banksia.

Derek W. Oakley, Perth

Derek and Sue are great friends of mine, and have a fine collection, built up over a number of years. I asked Derek to share some of his background with us.

"I started bonsai in 1985, after meeting a lady physiotherapist. After my treatment, we talked and she suggested that I try bonsai. She gave me a book written by an Australian couple. I read it and was hooked. There was not a lot of knowledge in Western Australia at that time, so we all seemed to bumble along. We had a few visiting experts, but our conditions are a little different to other climes. We are very much like California, except that our water is better, as Ernie Kuo told us when he was here in 2001.

"I have been concentrating on Australian natives since 1998. I find they respond well to cultivation. My son has a small farm in the southwest of our state with quite a few different species, and he lets me dig one or two. I also have a license to collect certain species that are not on the endangered list (only by bulldozers). Melaleucas, or paperbarks, form a large part of my collection. I have been doing some research and have found that most of them shoot back better if you break, rather than cut, especially larger branches and trunks. Also, a little heat from a blowtorch (used very carefully) stimulates them into new growth. The other tree of interest — and, surprisingly, it came from Ernie Kuo — is *Casuarina*. We have quite a few species, commonly called "she-oaks." At the moment, it is early for us, but in Hawaii, they have been using them for years and grow them like black pines, much quicker, though. Again, we have found them to be very forgiving and easy to collect, provided that you care for them after collection."

Derek won the BCI President's Award for best in show at the AABC convention in Fremantle 200, given by Lindsey Bebb on behalf of Solita Rosade, president of Bonsai Clubs International.

Liquidambar, 2004.

Liquidambar styraciflua (sweet gum). (TS, 1990, 36 inches [91 cm].)

Ficus benjamina. (TS, 1995, 33 x 24 inches [84 x 61 cm].)

Melaleuca. (TS, 1995, 29 inches [73 cm].)

Derek Oakley's winner of the BCI President's Award, 1999.

Melaleuca. (TS, 1995, 29 inches [73 cm].)

Ficus rubiginosa. (TS, 1987, 30 inches [76 cm].)

Melaleuca bracteata x "Golden Gem."
(TS, 1985, 24 inches [61 cm].)

Melaleuca. (TS, 1995, 40 inches [101 cm].)

Ulmus parvifolia. Bottom layered of the
top tree.

Collection of mame elms.

Liquidambar styraciflua. (TS, 1988, 40 x 28
inches [101 x 70 cm].)

Melaleuca, 30 inches [71 cm]. Since 2002.

Melaleuca. (TS, 2000, 33 inches [84 cm].)

Sue Oakley and mame. (TS, 1991,
2 inches [5 cm].)

John Di Vincenzo, Perth

John is one of Australia's fine bonsai artists, and has created a good-quality collection of Australian native trees as bonsai. John has been into bonsai for many years, and his trees are very elegant. These are just a few from his collection.

Pink *Diosma coleonema rosea*. (TS, 1989.)

Ficus rubiginosa nebari. (TS, 2000.)

Ficus rubiginosa. (TS, 2000, 28 inches [72 cm].)

Buxus microphylla (box). (TS, 1998, 32 inches [82 cm].)

Pink *Diosma coleonema rosea*.
(TS, 1994, 20 inches [50 cm].)

Juniperus procumbans nana. (TS, 1994, 32 inches [82 cm].)

Pink *Diosma coleonema rosea*.
(TS, 1989, 28 inches [70 cm].)

Ficus rubiginosa. (TS, 1987, 26 inches [65 cm].)

Cprosma kikii. (TS, 1990, 17 inches [42 cm].)

Melaleuca. (TS, 1995, 40 inches [101 cm].)

Paul Lee

Paul specializes in *Bougainvillea*. When I photographed his trees, he was in the midst of moving his nursery. Although photographing was difficult, I thought that his superb trees were worth photographing anyway. He has now opened his new establishment near Megumi Bennett's nursery (see page 102).

Pinus thunbergii (black pine).

Bougainvillea 3.

Ficus retusa.

Bougainvillea.

Bougainvillea 5.

Ficus rubiginosa, photographed growing on a mangrove stump.

Bougainvillea 2.

Ficus.

Ray Nesci.

Ray Nesci

Ray Nesci and his family run one of the tightest and most professional bonsai nurseries in Australia. It is extremely clean and very well maintained. Ray's selection of pots, tools, and books are world class. He has a huge stock of very interesting species, and specializes in bringing on field-grown material for bonsai artists. He has developed a new strain of elm that should prove a winner for those fortunate enough to obtain one. His son, Clinton, is a very talented artist in his own right. Of course, he has a great teacher in his dad!

Ray Nesci's new Hokkaido elm "Strong" variety.

***Acer buergirianum* "Nesci."**

Nesci Nursery stock.

***Acer buergirianum* 2.**

Megumi Bennett

Megumi Bennett is a Japanese-born bonsai artist. With her husband, Brian, and son, Alex, she runs Bonsai Art Pty Ltd and the Imperial Bonsai Nursery in Terry Hills, outside Sydney. Megumi has studied with some of the leading bonsai artists of her generation, and Alex was apprenticed to the famous Mansei-en Nursery in Omiya, Japan, owned by the Kato family. Both Megumi and Alex are university-qualified horticulturists. Megumi is also a well-known ikebana sensei, as well as a bonsai master. I have given classes in pine and satsuki at this excellent nursery, and enjoyed the company of the enthusiastic group of students who are regulars under the guiding hand of Megumi. Alex visited me in the UK and shared some of his considerable knowledge to help to improve my trees. All I now need is for his mom to show me how to make her amazing *goyoza* (dumplings).

Spruce group. (MB.)

Spruce group by Alex Bennett, 2004.

***Prunus persica* (peach). (MB.)**

***Chaenomeles japonica* (flowering quince).**

Craig, Megumi and Alex.

Kika seki chrysanthemum stone (biseki, polished).

Alex with some of Craig's bonsai.

Kika seki suiseki (biseki). (From the Bennett Collection.)

Sid Reeves with a mame elm.

Sid Reeves

Sid has been growing bonsai for much of his life. A superb technician, Sid has some very high-quality bonsai in his unique collection. I was privileged to spend time with Sid, and to be able to share these images with you. From tiny, mame-sized trees and landscape plantings to quite large junipers and paperbarks, Sid's trees are excellent examples of Australian bonsai.

Juniper-on-rock landscape image made by Sid.

Juniperus procumbans **informal upright.**

Juniperus procumbans **slanting bonsai.**

Juniperus procumbans **semi-cascade bonsai.**

103

Other countries

Japan

Masahiko Kimura

Masahiko Kimura is probably the best-known bonsai master in the world. He has consistently achieved the very highest awards for bonsai in the major exhibitions in Japan, and has created some of the world's outstanding bonsai. A great innovator, Sensei Kimura has shown us new ways to create bonsai, and has done since the mid-1980s. He has allowed some of his exceptional bonsai to be shown in this book.

Sensei Kimura's explosion into the world of bonsai was through his book, *The Magic of Kimura*. The exceptional designs were inspiring to a world that was jaded by "basic" techniques and wanted something more. It is curious that as we progress as bonsai artists, we also realize that learning the basics is always the best way to progress to other things. Mr. Kimura calls himself a "bonsai technician", and he is certainly that, as his wiring, carving, and innovative techniques are able to deliver such magnificent creations. He is much more than a technician, however, as he has traveled the globe sharing his expertise and friendship with bonsai enthusiasts in the many countries that he has visited. His friendship with Salvatore Liporace in Italy led Salvatore to new heights in design and he, in turn, has sent students to Mr. Kimura to serve apprenticeships. This has resulted in some outstanding bonsai artists coming into the teaching mainstream. These are some of his famous, award winning creations, which are synonymous with his excellence, and I am indeed happy that he has agreed to share them with us.

Shimpaku, *Juniperus chinensis* **var.** *sargentii.* **(MK.)**

The famous "Dancing Dragon," winner of the Prime Minister's Award, 1988. (MK.)

Jin of "Dancing Dragon." (MK.)

Body of "Dancing Dragon." (MK.)

Shimpaku, *Juniperus chinensis* (awarded the Sakuhu-ten Prime Minister's Award, 2000).

Shimpaku, *Juniperus chinensis* var. *sargentii*. (MK.)

Shimpaku, *Juniperus chinensis* var. *sargentii*. (MK.)

Spruce group. (MB.)

Goyomatsu, *Pinus parviflora*. (MK.)

Shimpaku, *Juniperus chinensis* var. *sargentii*. (MK.)

Shimpaku, *Juniperus chinensis* var. *sargentii*. (MK.)

Spain

Marbella Bonsai Museum

I first met the late owner of the Marbella Bonsai Museum, Miguel Garcia, back in the early 1990s. My parents had lived in Spain for many years, and the museum was just a few minutes from them along the road to Marbella. My father, who was a fluent Spanish speaker, took me to the museum and we found some lovely, old bonsai on display. I recently took my friend, the great Italian master, Salvatore Liporace, and his wife, Alessandra, there when they came to stay with me in Spain, and he, too, was impressed by some of the trees there. Salvatore is creating a bonsai museum in Italy, and this gave him a few ideas. The museum, now run by Mrs. Garcia and her son, is deservedly considered to hold one of the best wild-olive-tree collections in the world. It includes historical specimens, such as the Chinese "Almez" (*Celtis australis*), which had belonged to the same Chinese family for five generations, and a yamadori olive bonsai, which is now three hundred years old. Many of the bonsai in the beautifully laid-out museum were originally collected near Marbella, from the surrounding mountains. One species, the Pinsapo pine (*Abies pinsapo*), is now in danger of extinction through a recent attack by a local fungus. Found only in the southern mountains of Andalusia and in the north of Morocco, botanists discovered that the Pinsapo pine (actually a fir) had been around since the Tertiary geological period — before the Ice Age! Like the ginkgo tree and the Wollemi pine from Australia, this is truly a dinosaur of the plant world.

Ancient olives. (MBM.)

Swamp cypress (*Taxodium distichum*) 1. (MBM.)

Estilo natural. (MBM.)

Fig cascade (*Ficus retusa*). (MBM.)

Fig (*Ficus retusa*) 2. (MBM.)

Ginkgo biloba. (MBM.)

Nebari olive. (MBM.)

Ficus retusa 6. (MBM.)

Podocarpus. (MBM.)

Maple (*Acer buergirianum*). (MBM.)

Bougainvillea glabra. (MBM.)

White pine (*Pinus parviflora*). (MBM.)

Fig (*Ficus*) forest with figures. (MBM.)

Chinese elm. (MBM.)

Ficus retusa 3. (MBM.)

Ficus retusa 1. (MBM.)

Ficus retusa cascade.

Ficus retusa 5. (MBM.)

Ginkgo biloba forest. (MBM.)

Mixed group. (MBM.)

Hawthorn (*Crataegus*) 1. (MBM.)

Pine (*Pinus nigra*).

Podocarpus 2. (MBM.)

Japanese privet, California privet (*Ligustrum ovalifolium*). (MBM.)

Maple on rock (*Acer buergirianum*) (MBM.)

Switzerland

Georg Reinhard

Georg Reinhard was the winner of the national contest "New Talent" of Switzerland in 1999. In 2000, he won the international contest "New European Talent." He was invited to be a workshop teacher for the fourth WBFF Convention in Munich, Germany, in 2001, and for the ABBA Convention in 2003. Since 1999, he has been publisher and editor of the most popular bonsai magazine in the German language, *Natur und Mensch* (*Nature and Man*). His work is second to none, and he is a very talented demonstrator and master.

Mugho tanuki, 22 inches (55 cm). (TS, 1997, GR.)

Pinus mugho yamadori, 26 inches (65 cm). (TS, 2001, GR.)

Picea abies yamadori, 34 inches (87 cm). (GR.)

Pinus sylvestrus, 31 inches (80 cm). (TS, 97, GR.)

ABBA demo, 2003.

ABBA demo, 2003.

ABBA demo, 2003.

ABBA demo, 2003.

ABBA demo juniper, spring 2004. (TS, 2003, GR.)

Belgium

The Gingko Collection

Danny Use allowed me into both his private collection and his extensive nursery, which is one of the world's top bonsai nurseries. Danny only deals in good-quality material, and that includes local European yamadori and imported specimens from Japan and elsewhere. His pot stock is huge, and he sells the very best in European and Asian potters. He is a generous man, kind and very quiet, but developing as one of Europe's top masters. His teaching is excellent, and he holds his audience like a magnet. His better half, Ingrid, is also an extremely knowledgeable artist, and both will make you welcome when you visit Belgium. I always have a happy time when I visit Gingko.

Danny Use with a Scots-pine bunjin. (Gingko Collection.)

Danny with a trident maple. (Gingko Collection.)

Pinus parviflora (white pine). (Gingko Collection.)

The entrance to the Gingko Collection in Belgium.

The Gingko Collection.

Taxus baccata. (Gingko Collection.)

Juniperus chinensis. (Gingko Collection.)

Juniperus communis. (GC.)

White pine. (Gingko Collection.)

Spruce. (Gingko Collection.)

Juniperus chinensis. (Gingko Collection.)

Maple beni seigen.
(Gingko Collection.)

Taxus (yew).
(Gingko Collection.)

Zelkova nire (broom)
at Gingko.

Juniperus rigida (needle juniper) at the Gingko Collection.

Hinoki cypress at the Gingko
Collection.

White pine at the Gingko
Collection.

Pinus parviflora at Gingko.

Clump-style *Acer palmatum*.

Larix (larch) group at the Gingko Collection.

White pine at the Gingko Collection.

Acer buergirianum at Gingko.

Trident maple at Gingko.

Fagus crenata (Japanese beech).

Fagus crenata.

Juniperus rigida at the Gingko Collection.

Juniperus rigida group at the Gingko Collection.

Root-over-rock *Acer* at the Gingko Collection.

Fagus crenata at the Gingko Collection.

Acer palmatum koto hime at Gingko.

Acer buergirianum.

Clump-style *Acer palmatum* seigen.

Acer palmatum, shi she gashira, at the Gingko Collection.

Moss gardens and trees at the Gingko Collection in Belgium.

England

John Armitage
— creating an elegant image from a San José juniper

John is one of the brightest bonsai artists emerging from the UK. He is a dedicated enthusiast and has been involved in bonsai for a number of years. Here, he designs an old garden San José juniper at the Association of British Bonsai Artists' event in Bath, England, "The Joy of Bonsai."

Before wiring, jins were made and the trunk was cleaned. (CC.)

The upper part was now being prepared for wiring. (CC.)

A large shari was created. (CC.)

The San José juniper being wired. (CC.)

Wiring the foliage. (CC.)

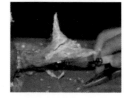

Detailed work was carried out on the jins using a chisel (ABBA.)

The final image was very elegant. (ABBA.)

113

The dinosaur tree

An ancient Wollemi pine.

The buds look like they can be plucked to create dense growth.

A recent discovery in Australia amazed and excited the bonsai world — the Wollemi pine, an ancient pine dating back to the Jurassic period, was found cloistered in a deep, unknown valley. It was accidentally discovered in the mid-1990s by a team of intrepid botanists from the Sydney Botanic Gardens. Its location remains a secret, but images illustrate the environment. The pictures show the pines in their secret valley, deep in the heart of the Blue Mountains. I was fascinated by this primeval landscape containing trees that I have never seen before. The Wollemi pine is one of the world's oldest and rarest plants. With fewer than a hundred adult trees known to exist in the wild, the Wollemi pine is now the focus of extensive research to safeguard its survival. The Botanic Gardens Trust of Sydney is now propagating these rare pines. They are fast-growing, dense, and have wonderful, unusual bark development. Only professional rock climbers can access the site, and we are grateful to the Botanic Gardens and photographer Jaime Plaza, of the Botanic Gardens Trust (Sydney), for the exceptional location images. Great efforts have been made to propagate the Wollemi for general use as an ornamental plant, and trials for bonsai are also being carried out. These first plants will become available in around 2005 or 2006 from the Botanic Gardens Trust (Sydney).

Wollemi pines in nature.

The foliage is almost like that of yew (*Taxus*). (CC.)

Wollemi pines in their secret gorge.

A Wollemi growing as bonsai material. (Sue Stubbs.)

chapter 4
design workshops

Techniques for design: to create a bonsai image, you must understand the various techniques of that design, as well as the source material.

Introduction

In this section, we look at the artistic development of a tree to create a feeling of age through carving.

A Colorado juniper with natural shari.

Shari-carving by Simon Temblett, North Wales.

A desert juniper with natural shari from the Dugger Collection, Atlanta.

Carving techniques
— carving jin and shari

Natural and man-made shari and jin

In this selection of images, you can see the wide variety of both man-made and natural defects that create the appearance of age in a bonsai. Whether it is the juniper stretching up to the sky at Arches National Park, or the creation of jin effects on an old larch, one teaches us the other.

Frank Hocking stands inside an old rainforest tree on the Great Ocean Road, Australia.

Desert juniper yamadori.

***Juniper communis.* Fifty years old, and three years in training to become a bonsai. (MABS)**

Shari on an oak.

Natural shari.

Jinned branches enhance this literati Scots pine.

Natural shari on a juniper in Utah, USA.

Natural shari on a buttonwood (*Conocarpus*) from Mary Madison, Florida.

Using a handheld router to carve detail. (Jim McCurrach.)

Carving an apex stump — yamadori mugho

Craig Coussins

It will take me five years to turn this four-hundred-year-old yamadori into a bonsai. This is but one step in that process. The tree has one branch and two lifelines. I need to reduce the heavy stumps where it was cut when collected without damaging the lifelines. The shari is wonderful, and I need to match that general look. I can detail it later. For now, I will reduce the stumps by carving — carefully!

Before carving an apex stump on the pine.

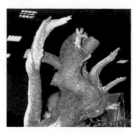

Carving an apex stump on the ancient pine.

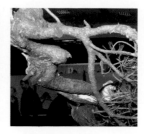

Two lifelines lead to the one remaining branch.

A close-up of the "stump."

Simon Temblett created the initial design for my tree.

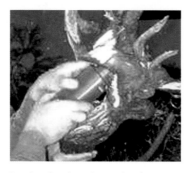

Carving begins. One mistake could kill the tree.

I needed to create a jin that looked like the rest of the tree's dead wood.

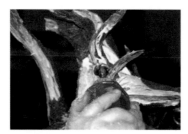

The detail had to be very precise. I used Samurai and Arbortech cutters initially.

I was working with old jins and new timber.

Reducing the mass to look natural needed every ounce of my experience as a carver.

This was eventually achieved.

I applied lime sulfur after wetting the wood.

The foliage was shaped. Here, you can see the natural shari.

The final result was much more natural.

Stump-carving

Alan Dorling, Wales

This is another example of how to reduce stumps by carving. Using the Arbortech extension arm, Alan Dorling, a very talented artist from North Wales, shows us the way.

Alan Dorling's yamadori hawthorn.

Carving with an Arbortech mini-grinder.

The carved image afterward.

The reduction of the stump.

Carving should look as though nature did the work, not man.

The stump was carved out with an Arbortech mini-grinder.

Carving techniques — Frank Mihalic

Frank J. Mihalic is one of the very few second-generation bonsai artists in the United States today. I met Frank some time ago, when I was working at his excellent nursery, Wildwood Gardens in Ohio. Frank has perfected his craft under the critical eye of his father, bonsai master Anthony (Tony) Mihalic. Anthony specializes in the rock and forest styles of bonsai known as saikei and yosue. Frank specializes in the single-tree styles more commonly associated with bonsai in the United States. Frank routinely travels to the Far East to perfect his skills with various world-renowned bonsai masters and growers. He is also the author of the first internet bonsai magazine in the world, (www.bonsaionlinemagazine.com). His latest book, *Bonsai for Kids Made Easy*, was recently published in French, German, Italian, Spanish, Japanese, and English. Buy it for the kids.

A cascade-style juniper with shari (dead-wood areas to show age).

Creating dead-wood effects on a bonsai tree

A close-up of shari and jins (dead twigs).

Shari and jin.

Carving tools for shari.

The generic name for dead-wood applications is the Japanese term *jin*. It is a dead and weathered branch on a bonsai tree that gives the illusion that the elements have killed or broken the branch, and that the rest of the tree has survived and kept on growing, aged by wind, rain, snow and heat. It really does not matter how old your bonsai is, only how old you can make it look! When we create a jin on a bonsai, we are trying to do two things: first, and foremost, we are trying to create the illusion of age; second, we are trying to create contrast between the weathered, whitish-gray jin and the brown trunk and green foliage.

A sharp knife for wood.

Creating an aged appearance on the trunk is called *shari*. It is a dead and weathered area, partially down, or along, the trunk, which can add a look of aged distinction, grace and aesthetic beauty to the tree. Sharimiki (stickleback) is where small jinned branches are left on the exposed trunk like fish spines.

Rough bark and wood removal.

Smooth out with grinding brushes.

A woodcarver's chisel set.

The Flex Cut chisel set.

What tools do you need to make a jin on your bonsai? You can use Japanese jin-scraper knives, wood chisels, sharp dental hooks or my favorite jin tool, one on a Swiss Army knife. (A new tool produced by Flex Cut looks like a Swiss Army knife, but all the blades are fine chisels.)

The first method is the traditional, Japanese way of creating a jin, which is to remove the bark and cambium layer of your tree's branch and then to use pliers to crush the branch and strip part of it away. This gives the illusion that the severe weather has eroded parts of the wood over many, many years.

After you have completed your jin, you will need to preserve it from rotting. Paint the dead wood with lime sulfur, which will preserve it. When the newly painted jin is exposed to the sun for a day or two, it will turn a chalk-white color. Many people use pure lime sulfur, and some use a white paint in combination with the lime sulfur. The grayish-white of the jin will give the illusion of a weathered piece of driftwood.

Clean shari with a wire brush.

Paint lime sulfur on wet wood.

LIme sulfur turns jin white.

The second method is a new way of creating a jin, using power tools. In this technique, you use grinders and wire brushes to create a more weathered look, where the wood has eroded and left deep grooves in the dead wood.

When you use a grinder on the jin branch, it will create very fine fibers of wood. Use a candle, lighter or small blowtorch to burn these fibers. This will create some black marks on your jin branch. Brush them with a wire brush before you apply the lime sulfur.

***Juniperus ibigana* shari.**

Lime sulfur turns shari white.

Keep lime sulfur off the soil.

Tips

- Many people use pure lime sulfur, and some use a white paint in combination with the lime sulfur.
- The lime sulfur will turn the jin a grayish-white color, like a piece of driftwood, after a while. If you add a little black sumi, or watercolor ink, it will turn the dried wood a more natural, gray color.
- Always use lime sulfur mix from a separate dish, and not from the bottle, otherwise dirt from the brush will contaminate the mix.
- Too much sulfur in the mix will make the first application slightly yellow or pale green, but that will later disappear.
- Subsequent applications will enforce the preserving qualities of the lime sulfur.
- Only apply lime sulfur in warm, dry conditions.

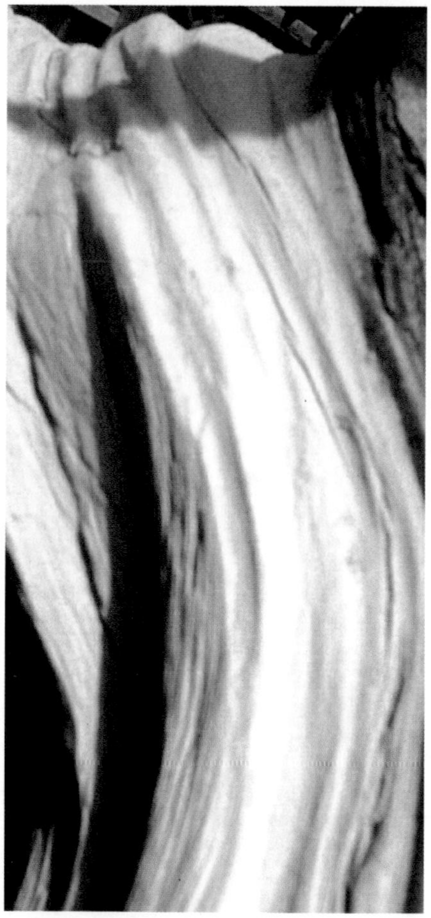

A close-up of a finished shari.

Lime sulfur stops wood rotting.

Jins and shari on *Thuja occidentalis*. (MABS.)

Moyogi-style juniper with shari.

Craig Coussins designs a hinoki cypress

This hinoki cypress (*Chamaecyparis obtuse*) was designed at the Mid Atlantic Bonsai Societies. The bush was grown as a garden plant, but was purchased to make a bonsai. I spent the previous day prepping the tree, wiring all of the branches and so on, which left me time to explain what I was doing and how I was planning to do it. I believe that many potentially good bonsai are lost when not enough effort is put into the demonstration. When I am privileged to be invited to a major event, I insist on having the previous day to prep large material and take the time to study it. The demo is not about showing off and making a bonsai suddenly appear in an hour: it's about creating art and making sure that the tree stays alive at the end of it. And perhaps entertaining my audience as well! I cannot achieve any of these aims if I am not sure what I want to do with the material. I enjoy finding the tree in the wood!

The hinoki cypress before its redesigning.

The top is removed.

The branches are wrapped in vet wrap.

Wiring the hinoki cypress.

The cuts are sealed after the main branches have been wired to avoid making a mess.

Always spray the foliage to reduce shock.

Heavy branch bends require latex tape and heavy wire.

Wiring the apex after the lower branches have been done.

You need a lot of wire for this art!

Wiring detail of the interior.

Shaping the profile of the lower branches.

I work on all sides throughout the process, and never just on one aspect.

Working in three dimensions helps the balance to succeed.

Nearing completion.

The completed back.

The left side.

The right side.

The completed front.

127

Craig Coussins

styles a yew

This tree is very straight and without really much in the way of branches. The apex was removed well before I saw the tree. It has an interesting top section that looks like fingers, where the clump of formerly living branches has, at some time, been cut back. However, this was not in my design plan. It could be a good tree, but it will need a lot more development of the foliage. There was no real structure in the available branches, and I had to find some way to emulate the appearance of a tree. I drew the image that I wanted to create and then worked on both the available foliage and the trunk. This is the initial styling into a formal upright, wind-blown mountain tree. That's the feeling that you should get from the design.

Craig Coussins with a collected yew.

The yew before styling, with hardly any structure in the branches.

An old cut would need to be dealt with by carving it out.

Its great nebari may determine the front.

I decided that this small amount of foliage would be my apex.

While interesting, this cut area looked odd, and I did not like it in my design plan.

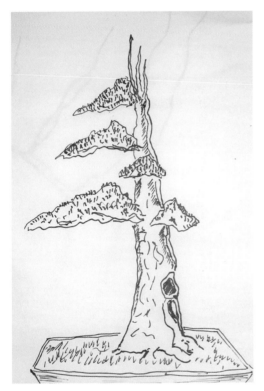

My drawing suggested a formal upright, slightly windswept look.

The sketch shows my plan.

Never wire the leaves upside down, or they will die.

I carved out the apex with a Samurai tornado.

The carving gave the tree the appearance of some age.

The carving needed refinement with a sanding flapper to smooth harsh edges.

The shari is where the old stump was.

Using cut paste to keep the edges moist allows the cambium to grow.

An image of the yew before its styling
provides a comparison.

The completed yew. The image looks
balanced all the way around.

The completed bonsai. Perhaps I will put it in a
pot in a year's time.

Carving a yew (*Taxus*)

Danny Use, Gingko Nursery, Belgium

(text and photographs by Craig Coussins)

Danny Use has emerged as one of the leading collectors and masters of bonsai in Europe. He hosts the prestigious Ginkgo awards and exhibition and runs the famous Gingko Nursery, Belgium, with his wife, Ingrid Van Lomel (see page 110). Here he is creating the first styling for an old *Taxus* that was grown for many years as bonsai material and, at present, forms part of the Gingko Collection. I photographed my friend Danny during the Mechelin Bonsai Convention in Belgium, where we were both headlining. I have huge respect for this man and his work, and am delighted to include him in this book. Danny took two Scot's pines from me a few years ago that I had styled at the European Bonsai Convention in Bruges. I called the intertwined yamadori literati "The Lovers." Since Danny has had them, they have evolved into a truly exceptional couple, and are both beautiful and elegant in their appearance of gentle and emotional togetherness.

Danny Use's yew (*Taxus*).

The other side of the yew.

Danny removing the flaky juvenile bark.

Cleaning off the flaky bark.

Danny choosing the new planting angle.

Cutting away the stumps.

Using trunk-splitters to create a natural "tear."

The stumps look more natural.

Danny explains that the dead trunk has no interest.

Using a die-grinder to carve out the trunk.

Carving dynamic undercuts.

As a result, the trunk now looks more natural.

Heavy wire is then wrapped with raffia.

Raffia is also put on the branches.

Danny trims down hard wood with splitters.

This is attached along the branch for extreme bends.

Carving out an area near the apex.

Wiring to all of the tips.

The side of the dead stump is now carved.

Danny now studies the options for the front.

Placing the branches.

Creating an apex.

The initial apex.

The apex will soon fill out on this *Taxus*.

All edges on live wood are sealed to promote cambium growth.

Carving A.

Carving B.

Carving C.

Carving D.

The front.

Danny with his bonsai.

The back.

Finding the wood in a tree

Craig Coussins

Informal upright — styling a yamadori Scot's pine

I was given this very loose-looking tree as a demonstration piece at a convention in Belgium. It was a collected tree, a yamadori, and while it had an interesting trunkline, the branches were very thin. It would have made a fine literati except for one thing — the vigor of the tree was suspect. I was not prepared to remove most of the branches, the obvious choice, as that could have damaged the already delicate growth of this thin, but old, tree. I removed the branches that I felt were not going to be part of the overall design, and then the two- and three-year-old needles that were still on the tree. This gave the new buds somewhere to develop, and allowed the application of wire by clearing the branches of unnecessary growth.

The application of wire was going to be a big job as the branches were very long and I needed to bring them into shape. I first wired the entire tree and made sure that each wire was secure and supporting each twig and branch.

Peter Lamoen, a superb architect and designer who owned the tree, was going to help me with this conundrum of a yamadori. The excellent and experienced Belgian bonsai artist Maria Hombergen also helped with the wiring. With three of us working flat-out, it took almost all afternoon. Normally, I prefer to wire the tree the day prior to the demonstration. Watching wiring is usually boring because the person wiring needs to concentrate and does not have much time to interrelate with the audience. However, with two such excellent assistants, I was confident that we could keep the audience interested. In fact, the audience was quite vociferous as some wanted me to drink more Belgian beer to help with the design process. I declined — I never drink and wire.

I removed a crossing branch at the base that was redundant to my design. I then started to shape the tree from the base upward. You always shape your tree from the base. If you styled the tree from the top down, you would get tied up in the lower foliage.

The tree turned out fine for its first shaping, although one person in the audience commented that she would have made it into literati. Although this was a perfectly valid idea, in my opinion, it would have killed the tree at this early stage. Maybe later, when the tree has recovered its health and vigor, we can look again at the styling. As a bonsai designer, my first styling for any tree is for its health, as well as its shape.

The yamadori Scot's pine (*Pinus sylvestris*) had a very thin structure.

I therefore needed to retain as much foliage as possible.

The pine was a little weak.

The needles were very small.

The two-year-old needles at the back needed to be removed.

This will allow new buds to grow, as well as space for wire.

Some branches need to be protected with raffia.

The raffia is required because the branches will be severely bent.

Raffia acts like a second skin, reducing fractures.

The preparation of wires, cut into lengths and wired in bundles.

Needles behind this and last year's were cut off.

Discussing the design with the owner, Peter. I always listen to the owner, and then to the tree.

I like to wire everything first to see what we have.

My team consisted of Peter Lamoen and Maria Hombergen.

It would have been dangerous to remove much foliage.

The thinner, second trunk was jinned.

The cleaned-up edges were sealed and jin wired into shape.

There wasn't much foliage — time to be a an illusionist again.

It would be a full-foliage pine.

The shaping started at the base and worked up to apex.

The apex was shaped last.

The branches needed to be shortened by bending them.

The edges were sealed and the jin wired into shape.

The apex was shaped.

The jin was wired into shape.

The right side.

The back.

The Scot's pine before it was styled.

The left side.

Yamadori initial styling

Lim Keow Wah

This is a slanting masterclass by Lim Keow Wah, of Singapore, the first styling of a yamadori juniper. Master Lim has, for many years, been conducting classes on bonsai and penjing at the Tanglin Community Club, Singapore, and has trained staff at the Jurong Gardens. Part of this wonderful collection is shown later in this book (see page 207). We contacted each other back in 1998 through our mutual delight in ancient Chinese bonsai pots, and I have now been to Singapore a few times. Master Lim had been collecting *Juniperus chinensis* in the mountains of China, and he brought some of these outstanding yamadori junipers back to Singapore. We worked on one of them at his home, watched by members of the penjing and suiseki club that Master Lim teaches.

Lim Keow Wah (LKW) collects mountain junipers in China.

Lim Keow Wah sits beside one such tree.

There is plenty of choice of mountain junipers.

In Singapore, prior to work.

Finding the front.

LKW cleaning out the foliage.

Creating another hollow area under the central dead wood, making it stand out.

The foliage was spiky, like juvenile foliage on cultivated *Juniperus chinesis*.

The foliage would have to be plucked to develop tight pads. This would be done now.

Plucking begins on the main foliage sections.

Club members and friends of the Singapore Penjing and Stone Appreciation Society were on hand to help.

The magnificent trunk had some damage to the natural shari, so a decision to develop this area was made.

A steel brush cleaned both the trunk and the dead-wood areas.

Excess wood was removed in stages from the area around the original shari.

The wonderful twist in the trunk would be enhanced by thinning this area a little.

The new old wood was then carved with a fine hook in order to create age lines in the newly exposed wood.

Branches that were not part of the design were removed.

The trunk was like a coiled snake.

The balance of the foliage with the trunk would now have to be made.

A length of wood was used to support the trunk while the work took place.

The tree needed to be brought forward and down.

The line of the tree would be in this direction to give a more dynamic image.

The wiring had to be very detailed and had to be carried to the end of each tip.

Now the wiring would begin.

Multiple wiring was used on most of the finer branches.

The branch that's covered will be removed in two years.

The first styling has been completed.

Club members helped.

Collected junipers.

Collected junipers.

Collected junipers.

Collected junipers.

Collected junipers.

A collected juniper after styling. (LKW Collection.)

A collected juniper.

The LKW Collection.

A collected juniper after styling. (LKW Collection.)

François Jeker designs a yew (*Taxus*)

François Jeker is one of France's leading bonsai masters. François was working here on a field-grown Japanese yew (*Taxus* var. *cuspidatea*) at the Association of British Bonsai Artists' (ABBA) convention in Bath, England. His work is exceptional, and I wanted to show you a great transformation. The demo took two days. The images are self-explanatory, but here is a précis of the transformation.

François started work on this yew in 2000 to encourage vigor, and two years later it was ready for this demo. At the ABBA event, he first cleaned out the back foliage to clear the branch lines. He then cleaned and washed the trunk and branches before moving on to the development of the jins (former branches that had already been cut off). He carved these into natural shapes and applied lime sulfur to the jinned areas. He then started wiring up the lower-section branches. Using latex self-adhesive tape on the larger branches to prevent damage, he wired everything, right down to the tiny twigs. The lower section was completed, and this was the end of day one. He had been working on the yew for nearly eight hours. (This is a fact that we, as bonsai artists, always try to explain: good bonsai-creation is not a one-hour transformation, and at ABBA events, we get two days to deliver a work of art.)

The next day, François worked on the upper section of the tree. He cleaned out the back foliage before wiring. After applying the self-adhesive tape, he wired everything. The main part of the tree took a long time to develop and the final result was astonishing.

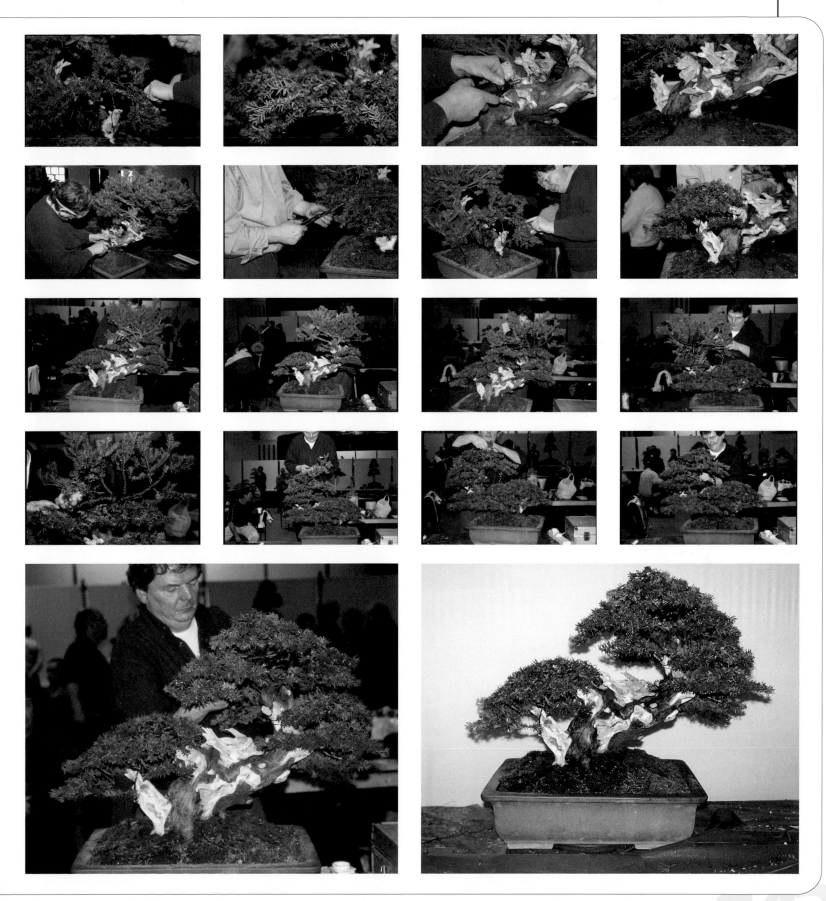

Inverted-taper solutions

Harry Harrington

Solving an inverted taper by splitting the trunk at the base

I collected this *Thuja occidentalis* "Aurea" a couple of years ago, from a garden where it had been growing for five or six years.

After allowing a year's recovery, I started to address the long branches that only had foliage at their very ends. I pruned the branches hard to create back-budding and slowly shortened each branch back to its new growth.

Having successfully split a thick branch earlier in the season to thin it (the first branch on the left, still wrapped in black tape), I decided to try splitting the trunk and opening it up to increase the taper at the base.

This technique is very stressful for any tree, but given the vigorous nature of this particular specimen, I felt that it had every chance of surviving. However, it was work that I wished to carry out before investing any more time in developing its branch structure.

Trunk splitting is not recommended for deciduous species, or species that are especially prone to rot, particularly if the exposed wood will be directly exposed to the soil.

Here's the tree last summer. As you can see, it has an inverse taper at the base, as well as a large wound where I removed a large branch.

Given the very straight trunk, I could only see this tree having a future as a formal upright bonsai, but the lack of taper, in particular the inverse taper at the base, made the tree look ugly.

I lifted the tree from its pot and cleaned the roots of soil. They had grown very vigorously since the tree's original collection. I found a path up the trunk that would allow me to saw it in half from the root base up, into the main body of the trunk.

For the whole period that the tree was out of its pot (around an hour), the roots were misted frequently to ensure that they would not dry out.

Given the need to work quickly and accurately, the trunk is sawn from below, using a reciprocating saw.

A clear cut was made straight through the trunk. Note that the cut was made between two major roots growing beneath each side of the shari.

A piece of bamboo was then slowly inserted from the bottom of the cut, gradually forcing the split to open. Great care was taken to prevent the split from continuing unabated up the trunk. The tree was then repotted, slightly rotated toward the right (with the bamboo still in place to hold the split open).

The shari was extended higher up the trunk to encompass another wound from a previous branch removal. The shari and the split were carved to create a more natural appearance, and the previous, small, first branch was jinned.

Over the past few weeks, the shari has been painted with a mixture of lime sulfur and black paint to exaggerate the hollow. For now, the tree will be allowed to recover, and the next few years will be spent developing the branching and foliage density. At the time of writing, the tree has budded out very strongly for spring. The only sign of weakness is in the first right-hand branch, just above the shari.

J.P. Polman styles a juniper with a shari

Jean Paul Polman is a Belgian bonsai master. Here, J.P. designs a short, but thick, juniper at the Association of British Bonsai Artists' event in Bath, England, in 2002. His demonstration shows what can be done with what looks like difficult material.

J.P. Polman's juniper before work starts.

The first step is the creation of an interesting-looking shari.

Using a series of knives and carving tools, J.P. removes the bark and exposes the juniper's heart wood.

Then he makes a slight channel in the edge of these cuts to allow the cambium to roll over into the hollow and lie flat, instead of rising up on the edge.

There is a small "muscle'" down the back of the trunk, which allows J.P. to make a thin shari that will emphasize that furrow.

The next job is to wash the trunk thoroughly, and to remove any juvenile, flaky bark to bring out the red of the mature bark.

While the trunk is wet, J.P. applies lime sulfur to the shari that he has created.

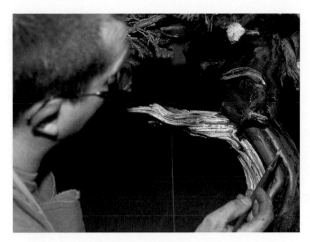

As you can see, all dead-wood areas have now been treated. This also has the effect of stopping any infestation of insects or fungi on the exposed areas.

The completed juniper. The foliage will soften in a year and the development will continue. A lovely example of a classic style.

J.P. brought along this beautiful example of a locally collected European black pine (*Pinus nigra*) that he had created.

The completed treatment needs to dry out overnight, so that is the end of day one.

The next step is to clean out the upper portion of the foliage in preparation for the wiring.

The apex needs to be created, so heavy wire and raffia are applied to part of the main upper branch.

Here you can see the new apical branch being pulled down, into shape.

Detailed wiring on the foliage needs to be carried out now.

It is important, on material like juniper, to wire to the tips of all branches, which takes time.

The side view, just prior to the tree's completion.

Landscape

Charles Ceronio

Charles Ceronio is one of the world's leading exponents of the African image in bonsai. Here is a series of pictures showing the creation of a landscape using trees to replicate the veldt image brought to the world by an important painter of southern African landscapes, Jacob Pierneef. Charles has taken that as a starting point for showing how to replicate an image from his part of the globe. You can study your own landscapes and do the same.

I first met Charles and his lovely wife, Elsie, back in the late 1990s, when I was the keynote speaker at the South African Bonsai Convention. We have remained friends ever since, and his present of a boot-shaped suiseki sits on my desk, reminding me that part of my company makes shoes for the Riverdance and dance companies. Charles started growing bonsai in 1968, and studied under John Yoshio Naka. He was the cofounder of the Pretoria Bonsai club in 1969, and in 1999 his book, *Bonsai Styles of the World*, was published to great acclaim. A headliner at many conventions, he travels around the world teaching bonsai, and has published articles on bonsai all over the globe. In 2005, he represented South Africa at the World Bonsai Convention.

In Charles' case study, he recreates what we call the "Pierneef image." This image is sparse, and the trees are in proportion, so they do not have to be large. The aim is to create an image that takes the viewer into the scene, using whatever materials will work. Less is more in this case. It's impressionism in bonsai.

I was introduced to Pierneef's work in 1966, shortly after he died. Although Pierneef did not have a particular image that he was known for, he had a style that he was readily identified with. For me, it is his sparse landscapes that come to mind here.

Piernaar's River (1945), by Jacobus Hendrik Pierneef (1886–1957)

Charles writes: "When discussing the Pierneef concept, we are looking at one of South Africa's most famous artists. Pierneef painted, among others, landscapes with thorn trees, or acacias, with their typically flattened umbrella crowns.

After studying some of Pierneef's sketches, I decided to develop a new kind of bonsai style for South Africa. We have our own, unique trees, landscapes and shapes, which are completely different to those in other parts of the world. I spoke about this new concept in 1980, at the first African Bonsai Convention, held in Cape Town. I called my talk, 'The winds of change – indigenous bonsai styles for southern Africa'.

I introduced five new styles to the audience, including the baobab style, the Pierneef, or umbrella-shaped, style and the flat-top style. I used the name Pierneef as the artist was an inhabitant of my own city, Pretoria, and I wanted to honor him as an artist. This style is not restricted to a single shape, but covers variations of the images of the trees that you will see on the African veldt and in mountainous areas. These shapes can be single, double, multiple, slanting or, indeed, any traditional bonsai shape, except the traditional triangular or pyramid shape, which is replaced by the flatter, or umbrella, tops of the African thorn tree, or acacia. So now when you see films of giraffes, zebras and buffalo in an African landscape, you may notice the differences in the outlines of the trees that surround the animals."

The Pierneef concept — from a lino cut.

A Pierneef-style image by Craig Coussins, based on Pierneef's *Landscape with Trees*.

The blue thorn tree, also known as the cat's claws thorn tree (*Acacia erubescens*), is exceptionally good for bonsai. The trees that we are using were grown at the Attie Louw Bonsai Nursery in South Africa.

Five trees were selected.

Setting up the material.

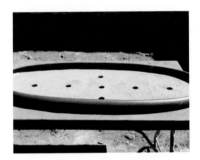

A 4 foot (1.2 m) fiberglass pot is chosen as a starter container.

The material in place.

Trimming out excess growth.

The completed African landscape.

Acacia bonsai. (ABA, DW.)

Acacia bonsai. (ABA, DW.)

Charles' garden.

Charles' garden.

An African landscape. (Photograph by Craig Coussins.)

A forest group created by Charles Ceronio. (ABA, DW.)

149

Monterey-pine styling

Craig Coussins

Refinement of an old pine bonsai that has grown out of shape

Next to the Scot's pine (*Pinus sylvestris*), European black pine (*Pinus nigra*) and white pine (*Pinus pentaphylla/parviflora*), one of the ten best trees for bonsai is the Monterey pine (*Pinus radiata*).

I worked on an old Monterey pine at Paul Sweeny's bonsai nursery in Melbourne, Australia. Paul had allowed me access to any tree that I required for this demo. My specialty is refinement and the recovery of older material, and this was a perfect example of what I prefer to work with. The tree needed cleaning up and the angle of placement needed to be established. It would be developed into a leaning style.

I first removed the two- and three-year-old needles and then fine-wired the tips from the closest twig divisions. Unless you need to move the branch itself, just wire the area that you need to work on. I needed to place the needles into foliage pads and some of the thicker branches were to be bent.

The following images show the progression to the finished shape.

I found this Monterey pine at Sasha-Eda Bonsai, in Monbulk, Victoria.

The first job was to remove the old needles. (The camera shows the tree's size.)

This Monterey pine's botanical name is *Pinus radiata*.

This tree had a good branch that I could have used as a "7" design.

I noticed its good branch structure and decided on a slanted style.

I thinned out the needles and started to remove the redundant branches.

The major wiring was done within an hour.

The fine wiring took me a little longer.

First the lower branches, then the apex — it was taking shape.

Tilting the image slightly helped its movement. The demo took three hours.

Natural examples of jin, shari, and uro

When we carve to give the illusion of age, we need to see where that inspiration comes from. Here are a few examples of one of the more difficult age features — uro (holes) on the trunk or branches. You need to undercut the cambium and then seal the edges. Keep the hole protected from water to avoid rot. When the wound has dried, paint inside the hole with either wood hardener (for soft wood) or lime sulfur (for hard wood). Color the surface a dark gray to black to give the illusion of depth.

Natural tree damage – the lower part has not healed (jin–uro).

Natural tree damage — curved-in cambium (uro).

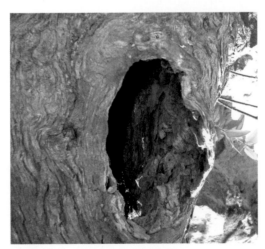

A thin-edged uro.

A swollen-edged uro.

An uro's dark center.

A hollow trunk and uro.

Recovering an old juniper bonsai

Craig Coussins

This old tree had been a bonsai for a long time. The owner, an excellent artist in her own right, was waiting for a visiting teacher to work on this tree – and this is what I created. It is a "7" style, which means that the branches angle downward from the trunk. If the upper portion of a tree is removed above the lowest branch, the result is like a seven shape. It's a natural shape.

This was one front. I liked this one.

A new literati had emerged. This is the other front.

I noticed that the lower branch was a "7" shape, which I liked.

I removed the upper part of the tree and wired the rest fully.

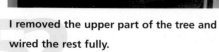

The juniper that needed refining.

The front.

Recovering an old pine bonsai

Craig Coussins and Ric Roberts

Ric Roberts, from Australia, brought this tree to a workshop. It had originally been designed by a visiting bonsai master some years ago, but the design needed updating and the tree needed repotting. I drew the new shape that I wanted to make, and although it was not a lot different from the original style, it was a great deal neater. I needed to angle the tree upward and replant it without causing too much root disturbance. We first wired the tree, and I designed the foliage pads. After this, we potted the tree at the better angle so that it now had two good viewing directions. I created two different drawings for alternative solutions. The sketches allowed the owner to see exactly what he was going to get and then make suggestions for changes. Ric knew me well enough and let me get on with it, although when I suggested that we might cut off the top and would then work from the bottom branch only, he blanched and chose this alternative refinement.

This old pine had grown out of its previous shape and needed restyling and refinement.

I tilted the image and then repotted the tree without cutting any of the root mass.

Now repotted, the tree had its old needles removed. Ric wired the smaller branches, then I reshaped the lower branch.

The completed tree, in its new pot and displaying its new angle. Now the image is balanced in an elegant informal-upright style.

Maple-group redesign

Ric Roberts and Craig Coussins

Ric Roberts is from Australia, and has been involved in bonsai for many years. A popular teacher and organizer, he is a well-respected member of the Australian bonsai community. Ric has a very large collection of superb bonsai, and when I visited it, I was amazed by the quality of some of these excellent trees. I was fortunate to be able to work on some of these bonsai when I visited, and in this example, I had the pleasure of working with this quiet master.

Ric has had this group for some time. First created using mature trident maples (*Acer buergerianum*), the group had been planted in a deep pot. The arrangement of the group was not working, so Ric decided that we should rearrange it and use a different pot to create a more realistic image. We had visited Orange, and had stayed with our friends Winnie and David Fong, who have a beautiful old house. During our visit, we went to Cook Park to see its wonderful avenue of English elms (*Ulmus procera*). The receding depth of this image was the inspiration for the maple group. Cook Park has a great collection of *Ulmus* that are sadly becoming rare in other parts of the world.

Ric Roberts did not really like the group and wanted to redesign the image. The group had no depth.

A magnificent avenue of English elms (*Ulmus procera*) in Cook Park, Orange, Australia, showing perspective.

Ric Roberts with the newly designed group of tridents in their new pot. The group now shows perspective.

How was this achieved? There was no depth or real interest in this placement, so reshaping was required.

The side.

Removing the maple group from the pot, which was too deep.

Making sure that the edge of the group has been cleanly cut from the edge of the pot.

Tipping the pot to remove the group of maples.

The group will now be planted in a smaller, shallower pot as the old one is too deep.

The roots in the soil mass are too dense. We can cut fifty of them.

Maples have feeder roots growing right up to the trunk.

The roots are very healthy, so they are now being teased out.

This is done quickly with a sharp pull saw.

Cutting the root mass will make it a lot easier to separate the trees from one another.

The soil is removed from each tree's roots.

Ric now cuts some of the interwoven roots. All cuts are sealed with Kiyonal.

The trees are now laid out individually.

The trees are now sized and, if necessary, some will either be changed, added to, or removed.

The bases of the major trees need to be leveled to sit better in the pot. All large cuts are well sealed.

Rooting hormone powder is applied to the edges of the large cut to aid root development.

Always keep the exposed roots and trees misted to prevent them from drying out.

Any large, bulky roots under good roots can be removed in this instance.

Always use sharp saws and shears when working with roots and branches.

Rather than removing some wayward roots, it may be better to wire them into a new position.

Larger roots that need to be moved can be cut slightly to allow bending when wiring.

To repot, first place sections of mesh over the holes in the pot.

Cut the mesh slightly to allow the tree's retainer wires to be inserted into it.

The wire retainers will need to be connected exactly for strength in holding the trees.

The soil is added and then the first tree is planted. This is the largest tree.

The second tree is planted. This is the next-largest tree.

The third tree is added.

The trees are now all tied into the pot.

The trees are placed to give the impression of depth.

The smaller trees are now added at the rear of the group to give perspective.

Turning the pot to see a side view to ensure that no tree is blocking another from view.

You can adjust the position of the trees by lightly wiring them to one another to secure them before moving them.

A detail of the surface. You can really see the depth now.

The completed maple group.

Garden juniper

Rob Atkinson

Rob has worked with me for years now. As a good friend, he comes up to Scotland from England and helps me with some of my more difficult and larger trees. He is a big man, with a heart of gold, and his artistry in bonsai is distinguishing him as one of the great masters of the future. In this example, he styles a *Juniperus chinensis* "Old Gold" that he rescued from a demolition site. There were a number of large, raised beds in this old building's forecourt, and they had to be cleared. Rob had less than twelve hours in which to lift these huge beasts. He managed to get four trees, but about another thirty were destroyed before he could lift them. When you look at this example, it will inspire you to go out and rescue potential bonsai from demolition workers. This is a great design, with a great piece of material. Rob heads up the New Zealand Bonsai Convention in 2005.

Rob Atkinson's *Juniperus chinensis* "Old Gold."

Carving out a stump.

Using a die grinder.

It's vital to wear a face mask when carving.

An angle grinder fitted with an Arbortech finishes off the job.

The trunk now displays a good line.

Creating jins.

A stump is removed near the apex.

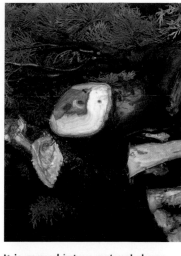

It is carved into a natural shape.

Sealing them with Kiyonal latex
keeps cuts moist.

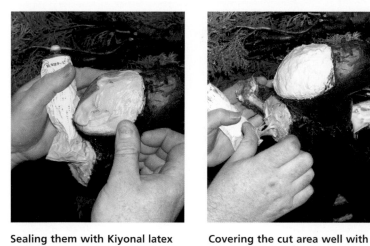

Covering the cut area well with
this new "skin" aids healing.

Wiring the tree.

Carving out a small shari.

The first branch is pulled down.

The branches are flexible.

The image is still looking rough.

Reducing the jins, which are too large.

Having realized that the side jin is too heavy . . .

. . . I have removed it.

Now the bonsai looks balanced.

The back of the bonsai.

Detail on the area of a former large jin.

Refinement of the back foliage.

The right side.

The left side.

The front.

Mugho-pine styling

Serge Clemence

Serge is one of Switzerland's rising young bonsai masters. He brought this old, collected yamadori to the Association of British Bonsai Artists' (ABBA) "Joy of Bonsai" convention. This was to be its first styling. As you can see, many large stumps were removed, and the foliage comes from pretty much one small area. A superb design.

Serge Clemence's *Pinus mugho* pictured in the year prior to work being carried out on it.

The mass of branches that was to be designed by Serge.

Working out from where to remove the stumps.

Removing the stumps with a power saw. Serge eventually had to use his considerable muscle power to saw through these ancient trunks with a handsaw.

Enhancing the furrows in the old trunk. The tree is probably around four hundred years old.

The line is now appearing.

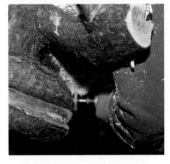

Refinement of the lower shari is done with hand tools.

This is the other side, and you can see the new line of the tree emerging.

To make this area look natural, Serge now cuts away some of the wood.

Serge then pulls strips down by hand to create thin furrows in the wood.

Using a sharp cutter, Serge continues to define the pattern.

Serge working on the almost completed area of shari.

Finally, to get the edge of the cambium to roll over, he uses a Samurai tornado to cut into the edge of the new shari at the edge of the bark. The cambium will now roll over naturally after he seals the edge.

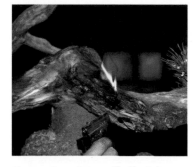

He needs to burn off all of the rough edges, giving the freshly carved areas some charred material to rub into the newly made, "aged" fissures.

It is not easy doing this near living tissue — be careful where your flame is operating!

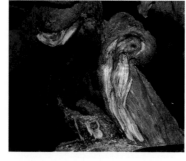

The previously carved shari has also been "burned," and the image is a lot smoother now that the detritus has been cleared from the wood.

A close-up of this area.

Serge starts work on the heavy upper part of the tree.

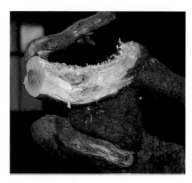

The thick stump needed to be reduced and shaped.

As he uses a Samurai tornado, this part of the design is quite fast, and a new, more slender, jin soon appears out of the thick stump.

Serge holds up one of the stumps that he has discarded.

The tree's form and line are now visible after all of the carving has been done and the jins have been burned.

Serge explains that the foliage needs wiring, but did you realize that the tree only had one branch?

The back of the "one" branch. This is the end of the first day, and so Serge applies lime sulfur to the new shari and jin areas, which will dry overnight in time for the next day's work — the creation of the foliage pad.

Wiring starts on the lower section of the branch.

Serge applies wire.

The lower branch is pulled into his predetermined shape for the lower part of the foliage mass.

The pads are laid out neatly.

This image shows the rough outline as the tree nears its completion.

Working from the front, Serge designs the apex.

The apex is almost complete, and you can see the foliage pads.

The completed four-hundred-year-old mountain-pine (*Pinus mugho*) yamadori. Designed by Serge Clemence, of Switzerland, and photographed by Craig Coussins.

Slanting to upright — a potting exercise

Craig Coussins

This is an example of a slanting, or cascade, tree that may look better in a more upright position. It is a very large tree, and I wanted to arrange the pot literally to scaffold the tree into its container for at least a couple of years.

A deep pot will allow for root growth.

Here, the tree is too low in the pot.

This is a good height.

Feeder roots and mycelium.

The framework holds the tree in place.

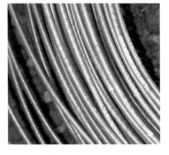

Covered copper wire stops copper leaching into the soil.

Securing the struts with wire and the tree to the struts.

Dry soil is added to fill all of the spaces.

The soil is a mixture of Kiryu, Akadama and grit.

The sides of the pot were tapped to fill any spaces.

The tree is now secure.

Watering it in thoroughly.

First styling of a twin-trunk juniper literati

Craig Coussins

This is really a demo piece that reads more like a wiring demonstration. However, the tree needed to have its apex elevated to make it a little taller, and this is the initial styling. The owner, Joy Morton, the New Zealand bonsai master, kept this tree for me after I saw it five years ago in her nursery during a teaching tour. Now that I was back, Joy brought the tree to the convention for me. It is an elegant image, although a little tall. I will suggest a slight change later for the final image. Removing the branch over the smaller trunk would result in a cleaner image, as would a slight reduction in the apex — this would help it to become a literati.

The *Juniperus squamata* "Meyeri" before styling. The tree is 39 inches (99 cm) high.

I also use vet wrap to protect the branches.

I will need heavy wires in order to elevate the apex.

I apply protective, self-adhesive tape over a thin cotton bandage.

I attach two wires along the length of the branch for additional strength.

I tie these onto the branch until it has been wrapped.

The *Juniperus squamata* "Meyeri" after its styling. The foliage pads will quickly fill in.

Larch: European larch (*Larix deciduas*)

Larch (*Larix*) is a lively tree. It is fast-growing and easy to develop as a bonsai. Only cut back the new growth in winter before bud-break. Cut back to the first of the two new buds on all twigs. That generates fine twig structure. Never cut the longer-growing fronds of growth in the summer period. That would slow the growth and stop the bud development. Larch is appreciated in the winter for its dense twig structure; in early spring, when the new buds open into tiny florets; in early summer, when the growth is dense and green; and in the fall, when the glorious foliage turns a bright yellow. It should be allowed to become shaggy in summer so that the buds can swell and get ready for the winter. European larch is a coarse tree, unlike Japanese larch (*Larix leptolepsis*), but it does have a much corkier trunk, which shows great age after about ten years.

Styling a yamadori larch

Craig Coussins

At a convention in Belgium, Erik Delanghe, an artist of exceptional ability, brought this collected tree for one of my demos. I first drew two alternatives for the design. The tree was a raft style, with two trunks growing directly up from the horizontal trunk. It will become a beautiful tree in about five years, after the ramification has been developed.

Always remember to leave growth in summer and to prune to the last two buds of this year's growth in winter. You then rub off the bud in the opposite direction to that in which you wish the tree to grow. You cannot do that if you keep pruning the tree throughout the year. Only prune once a year in late winter. After this demo, Erik and I pruned out some more foliage to help to give more definition to the structure, and that will develop in around two years.

In the two larch-forest images of my own trees, you can see a summer and winter image taken in the same year.

Larch group, 36 inches (92 cm) tall, 31 inches (80 cm) long, years in training: twenty. (Craig Coussins.)

The demonstration larch before its styling.

The front.

Long nebari on the larch.

The right side.

The back.

The left side.

I drew two versions with one and two trunk options.

The owner mists the foliage.

Some branches were protected with vet wrap.

Wiring to the tips. Wire over soft foliage if a tree is deciduous.

The front of the yamadori larch.

The yamadori larch and the team: Erik Delanghe, Maria Hombergen and Craig Coussins.

All branches were wired.

The branches were now bent into my design.

Leaving two trunks or one?

Now I work on the apex.

The tree is taking shape.

The back (alternative front).

The right side.

The left side.

Styling an old *Thuja*

Craig Coussins

Eastern white cedars (*Thuja occidentalis*) are native to eastern Canada. These trees have similar foliage to the hinoki cypress, but have a more open scale structure. They are not cedars, in the sense that they are not related to the true cedars. They develop shaggy bark, and when old, natural, dwarfed trees are collected from their native territory, they often have, like junipers, areas of dead wood. Eastern white cedars like a lot of high-nitrogen fertilizer, starting in the first part of the growing season and continuing until the end of mid-summer. They are a colder-climate species that will not grow in hotter climates.

My demo *Thuja occidentalis* was in a mother-and-daughter style.

Although a small tree, it was a very old specimen.

I thought that this would be my best viewing angle.

The bark was peeling and the shari and jins were natural.

An aged shari suggests that this tree may be over a hundred years old.

After some thinning out and light wiring, this was the preferred front.

After some thinning out and light wiring, this was an alternative front for the tree.

In all of my designs, I try to balance the bonsai all the way around.

This was the other side of the *Thuja occidentalis* (which was owned by Linda Brant).

An eastern white cedar group by Reiner Goebel.

Dead-wood effects in nature

When designing bonsai and penjing, we must always look at nature for inspiration. It is much easier to refer to an image that you have seen than one that you have never seen. On my travels, I photograph almost anything that I find either unusual or interesting as a bonsai artist and teacher. With over 52,000 species of trees to discover, I will not run out of material. While my photo library now exceeds half a million images, covering everything from bonsai to landscapes, I still like to add to this resource so that I can show others these amazing images from Mother Nature.

Burrs and cankers create interesting textures on this tree trunk in North Wales.

The dead wood on this Utah juniper has an almost black-gray appearance.

Some of these images are more than interesting as we come to Tony Tickle's section on dead-wood carving by sandblasting. I have included some shots of Bryce Canyon bristlecone pines to go with his examples. Although they are not the truly giant, wide, bristlecone-pine images that you may have seen before, they are more approachable, in the sense that they are very old trees, but still have good, vigorous growth. Bristlecone pines are not supposed to be living, but rather constantly dying. Bryce Canyon bristlecone pines are no exception. In Bryce Canyon, Utah, the sand has polished the dead wood on these junipers to a metallic silver. Tony Tickle looks at trying to achieve the smooth, but aged, appearance of ancient trees, and these images reflect his ideas. Tony was just off for three weeks' canoeing, trekking, and hauling camera gear to the Grand Canyon National Park when he sent me his section for the book, and will no doubt photograph any amazing yamadori that he comes across there.

Jins form part of the tip extensions, as well as the bark, on this acacia wattle tree that I photographed in Australia.

I found this huge cavern in an old beech in a rainforest on the Great Ocean Road in Australia.

An old juniper on the edge of a sulphur lake in Yellowstone, Wyoming. The living tissue still clings to this natural bonsai.

A shari similar to the one in Serge Clemence's demo, where he burnt the shari to create depth.

A Sherwood Forest oak with an unusual, hollow trunk that has regrown around old damage.

Shari and uro are visible on this old oak (*Quercus*).

This oak sports an interesting repair on its trunk, perhaps covering a branch lost half a century earlier. Jins also abound.

This tree has grown up through an old hawthorn; the remains of the original tree are at the front.

The apex of a Sherwood Forest oak tree.

Shari and a hollow trunk on another oak.

The nebari shows an interesting shari formation.

Shari being grown over on an old mountain mahogany, Great Basin National Park, Nevada.

A giant *Sequoia* in Yosemite, California, the trunk showing fire damage and a consequent hollow. *Sequoia* need fire to propagate their seed cones.

An old juniper in the Great Basin Desert, Nevada, under the snow-capped Sierra Nevada range. Constant cold and searing heat cause die-back.

This old Scot's pine in the north-east of England has lost one side of its trunk and now looks like a natural bonsai.

Perched on the edge of a gorge, this bristlecone pine is in Bryce Canyon, Utah.

Ancient pines on the top of Half Dome, in Yosemite, California.

Covered in jins, this majestic, foxtail bristlecone pine (*Pinus longaeva*) is in Bryce Canyon, Utah. The other species of bristlecone pine is *Pinus aristata*.

The foxtail bristlecone pine's bristles look like foxtails, hence its common name.

A bristlecone pine at Yovimpa Point, on the Bristlecone Loop Trail, Bryce Canyon, Utah. It is estimated to be over 1,600 years old — a mere youngster.

In recent years, there has been a distinction made between the two species of bristlecone pine: *Pinus longaeva* is commonly called the Great Basin bristlecone, while *Pinus aristata* is the Rocky Mountain, or interior, bristlecone. *P. longaeva* grows at Bryce Canyon.

Creating "dead-wood" effects on bonsai

Tony Tickle, England

Tony Tickle is one of those guys whom you cannot help liking. He is a marketing guru, with a successful advertising agency, and his artistic ability has made him a very successful businessman. He has always been kind to me, and ready to say "yes" when I ask him to help me. Over the years, Tony has emerged as a great designer of bonsai, and he specializes in collected yamadori. He is an excellent bonsai teacher, as well as an artist, and I am sure that we will see much more of this very talented and highly intelligent man.

In the search to create bonsai that are mature and aged in appearance, I am prepared to go to extraordinary lengths. Here, I concentrate on the creation of natural-looking, aged, dead wood.

Bleached dead wood is a natural phenomenon on ancient mountain trees, such as the bristlecone pines (family: Pinaceae; genus: *Pinus*; subsection: Balfourianae). There are three species within this small group: the Rocky Mountain bristlecone pine (*Pinus aristata*), found in Colorado, New Mexico and Arizona; the Great Basin bristlecone pine (*Pinus longaeva*), which is sometimes also called the foxtail pine, found in Utah, Nevada and eastern California; and the foxtail pine (*Pinus balfouriana*), found in California. These trees are often thousands of years old and display copious amounts of dead wood.

Old yew trees in exposed locations exhibit wonderful, white or silver dead wood. But unless you are lucky enough to have access to old yamadori, creating that authentic, ancient, dead-wood look is difficult and requires specialist tools.

Over the last few years, many bonsai artists have been creating "dead wood" using electric carving tools, chisels and even fire! And some of the results appear very convincing. Yet however great the skill used in all aspects of styling and horticulture, the effort is wasted if the viewer is aware that the bonsai has been "carved."

Sandblasting trunks for definition

In 1992, I started my search for the creation of "perfect," authentic "dead wood." How is dead wood created? What happens to the live wood that is left? I went back to nature and found the answer . . . weather, sandstorms, high winds, rock falls . . . all that I had to do was to re-create these conditions, and my search would be over!

The answer was sandblasting — it had high winds, sand and, perhaps more than anything else, it was controllable, as long as you took precautions to protect the parts of the tree that were to be left unaffected by the process.

The material used here is a San José juniper. The original tree was field-grown by Dan Barton, and the original creation of the shari was performed in a one-to-one with Dan ten years prior to the final styling and blasting work on the dead wood.

This bonsai has been created over a period of twelve years (seven in the ground). During that time, the thickening of the lifelines created robust "tubes" of deep-red bark.

The foliage was left to grow long every three years, then cut back hard. All the time, the emphasis has been on a compact crown and good branch structure. San José juniper is notorious for only having foliage at the ends of branches because no light is able to penetrate the tree close to the trunk. The tree was lifted from the field so that the nebari could be checked and adjusted if required.

After ten years, I chose to style the tree at the Belgian Bonsai Association's annual show near Antwerp, Belgium, with the dead wood being further extended. The style displayed was considered many years prior to the demonstration.

Creating an ancient look on a nursery tree that is only fifteen years old

1. The original creation of the shari with Dan Barton. This work was carried out over the winter months, so the tree was tightly wrapped with nylon wadding to protect it from frost and allow it to callus well. The nylon wadding was removed after a full growing season. Here, Dan is initially positioning branches to create movement close to the trunk.

2. After seven years of growing in my field, the tree was transferred to this plastic pot. The soil mix was very open, and the tree was heavily fertilized.

3. The lifelines are very pronounced; this adds a great deal to the aged look.

4. It is important to start with good material if you wish to create a dynamic end product.

5. Ten years of cutting and growing and cutting back hard every three years have created a dense crown, excellent movement and natural taper.

6. The tree at the end of the Belgian Bonsai Association demonstration. Hans van Meer helped with the wiring and repotting into an Ian Baillie pot. The audience was quite surprised that I worked on the top of the tree and the roots at the same time. The tree was very healthy, and because I had worked at it for so long, I knew the exact condition of the roots and just how much I could remove.

7. Back home in my garden. The position of the tree is now fixed. Hessian is used to cover the exposed root at the back of the tree; because the planting angle was changed, the root ball was left exposed. Sphagnum moss was used to ensure that it stayed moist. It was left in position for eighteen months. The nebari was improved when the moss was removed.

8. The nebari eighteen months later. This still needs improvement, but there are no roots crossing, or any growing at an unusual angle.

9. The lifelines are very powerful; this gives a great feeling of age. Getting the dead wood to appear ancient alongside these lifelines is the objective.

10. All areas of the tree that are to be "aged" are left exposed. All other areas must be protected because the process is very aggressive. Here, I use a brass wire brush to removed flaky bark so that I can paint on a rubberized solution to protect the live wood from being damaged.

11. Painting on the rubberized solution. This is the best technique for protecting all areas. You can also use Plasticine, but ensure that it is warm when applied because it will then stick better.

12. Using this technique enables fine detail to be "aged".

13. Plaster of Paris is used to protect the soil and pot.

14. Carpet tape creates a seal between the plaster and protects the edge of the pot.

17. Inside the blasting unit. Very fine sand is used at a pressure of 110 psi. This gives the best balance between removing the softer wood and keeping the detail. A tree of this size usually takes about an hour to complete in the blast box.

15. The foliage is wrapped in tough plastic bags and the edges are sealed with tape.

16. The dead wood is all hand-tooled and stripped. The rougher, the better! I only use power tools to remove bulk, and the final working is done by hand.

18. A transformation in the finish of the dead wood — replicating nature by shortening the weathering process.

19. The rubberized solution simply peels off, although it does take a long time to get back to a nice, "clean" trunk with all the bits off.

20. The live part of the tree has not been touched by the blasting. The rubberized solution gets into every area, and the blaster can get in close to the live wood without causing damage.

21. When you look closely at the detail, it is hard to believe that this dead wood is man-made.

22. The top of the tree is created. All of the main branch placement has been created over the last six years, so in the final styling of the tree, no thick wire was used.

23. The wiring and removal of unnecessary foliage is to encourage growth by allowing light to reach the inner branches.

The tree has now had its final styling. This photograph was taken on the first day that the tree could be called a bonsai. It has many years to spend in development before it is in "show" condition. The tree needs to mature in foliage, and the dead wood must develop a patina that only age will give. All of the work done over the last twelve years was to "age" the tree prematurely in the eye of the viewer; the creation and placement of branches, the early establishment of the shari and the constant improvement of the nebari complete the picture. This tree is only fifteen years old, but I hope that it looks much older, and that, with time, it will look ancient.

24. The nebari is improved by removing small roots that cross major roots. The soil surface is dressed with a mixture of "Fuji grit" and Akadama. Moss is placed to add color and interest.

Tony Tickle with his sandblasted San José juniper.

"Twin Dragons" large yamadori styling: refining an ancient pine

Craig Coussins

I first saw this tree back in 1980, when I was trekking up the side of a mountain, pushing a wheelbarrow through 3-foot (1-m) -deep snow. I was with a friend, Jim McCurrach, with whom I worked through the 1980s while developing my bonsai skills. I had bought some yamadori pines from Jim, but I intended to lift a very large, old *Juniperus communis*. On the way down, I spied this pine and took some photographs. Jim cut the top down and we left it *in situ* for a year.

Jim then went back up the mountain and lifted it. We shared the tree for a while. I had it for four years, and then Jim styled it at one of our own conventions in the early 1990s. He planted it in his rockery as a feature tree, where it grew out of shape. I rescued it in 2001 and brought it back "home." This is the result.

The tree was deep in snow on the side of the mountain track, and I noticed it on our way down in the early evening.

Jim thought that it was too big (he was right), but I insisted that it had great potential.

We cut out the leader trunk and some of the side branches and left it for a year.

Fifteen years later, Jim had decided that it was too big for him as a bonsai, and had placed it in his rockery. I decided that it needed a better home, so I asked Jim to sell it to me. He was not pleased about losing his lovely rockery tree, but he knew my long-term connection with his tree, and that I really wanted to work on it.

This image clearly shows the potential of the pine, which is why I wanted to develop it. I began work on the tree two years later, in 2003, once the foliage had been increased.

I called it "Twin Dragons." Here it is in July 2003.

Trimming out the old needles.

The other side.

Kevin, Alan and Simon helped.

The inner buds were brittle.

Some branches were redundant.

Aphid damage on twigs
weakened the tree.

The branches needed thinning
out to my design.

We thinned out the structure.

One trunk had little foliage.

A bare tree in 2003.

Now the wiring starts.

After removing some branches.

On an adjustable-height table.

Alejandro Bedini, from Chile, dropped in to help us.

The following week, Rob and members of his club helped me to wire everything.

Rob helps with the detailed wiring of the tree.

Using a turnbuckle to move heavy branches.

The Twin Dragons a year later, in July 2004, to be dropped down into a new pot in spring 2005 (three years' work).

Maples

Maples (*Acer*) are one of the most popular genera grown for bonsai all over the world. In this section, we look at one of the most innovative techniques for maple-bonsai creation that I have ever come across: maple fusion. There is another, similar technique that uses *Ficus*. Essentially, these are the only two major tree genera that are easily fused.

While not all climates are suited to maple, it still accounts for the majority of bonsai in temperate climates. Many growers, no matter where they live, try to grow maples as bonsai. The finely twigged structure in winter is magnificent and entirely indicative of a full-sized tree. The spring and fall foliage is magnificent, and very colorful. The dense summer foliage again mirrors that of a full-size tree, and is one of the reasons why people choose maples.

Although the red-leaf cultivars, such as "Deshojo" and "Seigen," are the prettiest because of their red leaves throughout the year, I suggest that you start with the hardier, green-leaved types, such as pure Japanese maple (*Acer palmatum*) and trident maple (*A. buergerianum*).

The dwarf cultivars, or "Yatsubusa" varieties, are more delicate, so do not leaf-prune these types unless you are sure that they can take it. Varieties such as *Acer palmatum atropurpureum*, the dark-plum-colored maple, are sometimes weak and not easy to back-bud. Do not leaf-prune this color group, which is deep red to purple. You develop this variety through bud-pinching.

There is one variety of maple that grows differently to most others — the popular "Kiyohime" (pronounced "Keeyoheemay"). These trees are very dense, but very strong at the sides, so keep the side growth down or the upper portion will die back.

Many deciduous trees like maples are at risk of leaf-burn if you put them out in windy weather in spring. Put them out when the young leaves have become firm and hard, and keep them in a sheltered area away from wind, if possible. You may have to build a simple shelter.

Watering

Water a maple to keep the soil damp. You will need less water in winter in a cold or temperate climate, but if you live in a humid area, trident maples may need regular watering until you force leaf-fall by cutting all of the leaves off. Reduce the amount of water slightly as the tree is unable to transpire through the leaves until the new leaves have set. Mist-spray it once a day during spring, and twice a day during summer, in the morning and early evening; mist-spray it once a day until the leaves start to turn in the fall. Do not waterlog the tree, by which I really mean giving it only a light misting.

Pests

Most deciduous species attract pests – everything goes for them. However, the most common problems are aphids, whitefly, blackfly and, depending on your area, caterpillars. (Although caterpillars are usually species-specific, some are just hungry.) Treatment is with systemic in most cases. Spraying directly onto the leaves may damage maples, but new pesticides have recently been brought out that do not damage leaves. Ask about them in your local bonsai nursery or plant-health office.

Feeding developing maple bonsai — young to mid-stage

Do not feed young to mid-stage maples until the leaves are open.

- Feed zero, or very low, nitrogen fertilizer during the lush, soft stage of growth.
- When the leaves start to harden, increase the amount of nitrogen that you feed.
- In hot summer months, reduce to zero feed as the trees are now less able to take up feed.
- After the peak, start feeding with low nitrogen as that builds strength into the wood.
- Do not feed after the leaves fall.

Feeding mature maples

If you want good fall color, you will need to use a pellet food, or else reduce the amount of nitrogen that you feed a mature maple completely, since that stops the bright color changes.

Pruning and ramification

The health of the tree depends on your ability to create more and more twigs, which, of course, hold the leaves, which allow the tree to breathe. This is called ramification. It just means creating a dense, fine, twig structure. The health advantages of more twigs and branches mean that increasingly fine root development takes place, and that the tree has a solid base to stand on. Roots also help to define twigs. Roots mirror the branches and twigs. A tree with plenty of fine twigs, buds, branches, and roots advertizes your artistic ability as a grower of miniature trees. On this artistic level, the appearance of a finely twigged, deciduous bonsai (or a dense pine) gives a feeling of satisfaction. Bonsai arose from the art of meditation and, as we all soon come to realize when attending to our bonsai, time quickly passes when you are working on these little trees. You will find that elusive inner peace in this gentle pursuit.

Main buds at the end of each branch

When new buds have developed, keep the end of that branch short or the sap will bypass the new bud to feed the strongest bud.

- To get smaller leaves, pluck out the center of the buds as they start to form. If you leave it too late, you will not produce that effect.
- You can continue, however, during spring, to pluck out the entire center buds on the branches that you are happy with as far as length is concerned. This will develop fine twigs.

Light and shade

If you keep the tree in the shade, the branches and twigs will grow very long between the internodes, or leaf stalks. That's fine for young trees, but not for mature trees.

If you grow the tree in bright light, rather than hot sunshine, the internodes will be short.

Fusing trunks to create a large tree

I came across fused trunks nearly fifteen years ago, when my friend Thuenis Roos, who lives near Pretoria, in South Africa, showed me a technique of making large-size trunks by pulling a bunch of smaller trunks together and binding them.

Eventually, the trunks fused together, forming a nice nebari and what was essentially a broom-style foliage section. A variation of this technique involves removing a slice of bark and binding the trunks with raffia to ensure a tight grafting of the trunks. Using this method, Thuenis could create large-trunk shohin bonsai.

This aside, nothing can compare with the achievement of Doug Philips, of California. He has gone the extra mile and has created a new technique with which to graft together many small, thinner trunks. Either using a frame or a wood-former, he has managed to discover a way of making huge-size trees by literally fusing these thin trunks together. On my travels around the world, I have seen a number of instances where trunks have fused naturally. These have always fascinated me, so I asked Doug to share with us the methods that he has used.

Thuenis bound these Natal figs (*Ficus*), which soon bonded to create a much thicker tree.

Here, Thuenis tied seedling figs (*Ficus*) together and shaped them into a more mature image to create a fig that fused together after three years.

Maple-fusion techniques

Doug Philips, USA

Introduction

What is a "fused-trunk trident maple"? It is one tree created from many.

The concept is to arrange many small seedling trees in a specific manner to create one larger, bonsai tree. The basic process used to accomplish this task is approach-grafting. The ultimate advantage is achieving a larger bonsai tree in less time, and for less cost, than when using conventional methods of growing. Having complete control over every step of the growing process allows the artist the ability to produce a tree with an exact size of base, shape of base, nebari, flare, taper, movement, height, branch quantity and location. The first fused-trunk trident-maple tree was created in July 1995. The original project was constructed on a wooden form that had been carved to a predetermined shape and size. More recently, and with much improved success, a copper-wire frame was used to hold the seedlings in place.

The pictures on the following pages show the evolution of the wire frame that was used for a tree constructed in January 2003.

- It was determined that there were not enough horizontal wires to hold the young trees adequately, so more wires were added.

- Home-grown seedlings are usually better than nursery stock for this type of project. The seedlings were dug up, washed and selected for size prior to starting.

- The seedlings were then placed on the wire frame two at a time until the frame was completely covered. The composition was then placed in a large container in a raised growing bed for faster development.

- As the seedlings grew together and fused, the long portions not tied to the frame were selectively discarded. Some new sprouts were selected to become primary branches and were wired into position. Other branches and sprouts were left on for a bit longer to do their job of fattening and fusing.

- Once the fusing was about 90 to 95 percent complete, the tree could be removed from the growing bed and oversize container and root work could commence, balanced with branch ramification and trunk refinement. Over time, the individual character of each tree smooths out and blends in harmony with the trunk.

The photograph on page 189 shows the present state of a tree that was constructed in 1995. There are a few scars, soon to heal, where redundant branches were left on the tree for too long, but I hope that you can begin to see the idea come to life.

New advancements are always being made in materials and techniques. The wire frame for the tree that I am currently designing is shown to demonstrate the higher level of frame refinement and design that has been achieved this year. This advancement should generate a higher-quality fused-trunk trident-maple tree in record-breaking time.

Wire frames

The wire frame has proven to be the best method of reducing the time required to fuse trees together. Wire frames are now more complex, and solve the problems associated with earlier, simple designs and the older, wooden forms. They also have other advantages over a solid wooden form.

- Firstly, placing the seedlings in closer proximity allows for faster fusing. The wire ties used for attachment to the wire frame are thinner than nails and tacks; also, the seedlings can slide closer together once wired to the frame. Fusing can occur in about one-third of the time taken with earlier wire frames and wooden forms.
- Secondly, there is access to the "inside" of the tree, which was not possible with a wooden form. This access is valuable at the time of construction, and in the future, should the artist want to thread-graft genetically identical material for uniform branching.

In addition, there are smaller advantages, such as less mess during construction and more control of design and attachment. Wire frames are also lighter in weight, and have much greater design flexibility than wooden frames.

Before making a wire frame, it is very important to plan the design. Every aspect of the future bonsai is up for your consideration and under your control. The choices made will have an impact on the final appearance, long-term feasibility and success of your tree. Making a list of specific qualities and attributes will help to guide your decision-making process. Your list should include, but not be limited to, bonsai style, type of plant material, plant availability and cost. Do not overlook decisions about the finished tree's height and width, trunk movement, branch locations, the type of bonsai container, the container cost, growing conditions in your area, the projected time frame from construction to show date, and the final weight of the composition.

The frames are made from new copper wire and are soldered together. Tools and supplies for a project like this are generally not too expensive. You only need copper wire, a mini-blowtorch, solder, wire cutters, and pliers.

When creating your frame, use your imagination. You could consider a very classical shape or a contemporary form, with flair and high drama.

Trident maple (*Acer buergerianum*) fusion techniques

Doug Philips

Doug Philips' introduction to bonsai was in 1986. In 1994, Doug started specializing in several species of plant material that were of particular interest to him. These were personally collected sierra and California junipers, local olive trees and bald cypress from Louisiana, San José junipers, small-leaf, dwarf olives, *prostrata* junipers from cuttings and last, but not least, fused-trunk trident maples. If he had two real favorites, they would be tridents and olives. Doug is a regular speaker at American conventions.

Here are the results of Doug's innovative research into fused-trunk maples.

The earlier wire frame.

Another view of the earlier wire frame.

The development of the earlier wire frame.

Making the updated wire frame.

Creating the updated wire frame.

In the process of making the updated wire frame.

Making the updated wire frame: a view of the underside.

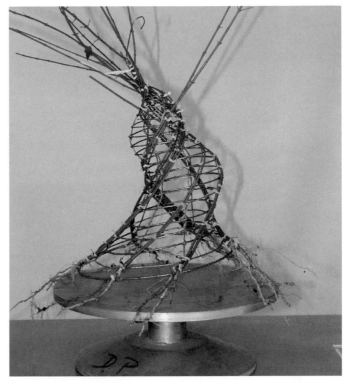

The seedbed growing ground.

A selection of seedlings.

Wrapping the seedlings.

Continuing to wrap the seedlings.

Wrapping the seedlings tied together in bundles.

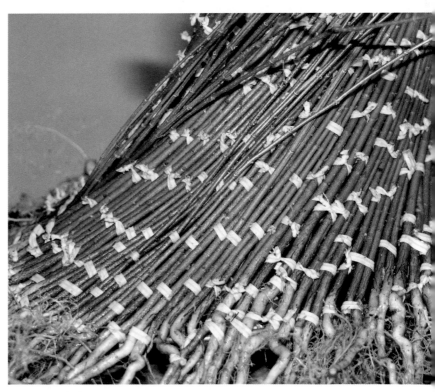

Wrapping the seedlings in stages to develop a complete mass by tying them to the frame.

A more detailed view of the wrapping procedure.

A close-up view of the seedlings in the process of being wrapped.

Inside the frame.

The seedlings are planted in a training pot of a good depth.

There is enough space in the pot for the roots.

The pot is dropped into the growing bed and drip-fed water.

This makes it easy to remove the frame and trim the roots.

The correct pruning produces tight growth in a short time.

The leaves are removed and the tips are pruned.

Improved growth and development in a later image.

A view inside the frame.

The original tree needs a repot.

The perfectly placed root system.

There is good development of the foliage mass.

A well-balanced specimen.

Despite some scarring, which will soon grow out, the trident maple has turned out well.

Defining the structure.

Nearing the final development.

Doug Philips' fusion maple.

Figs (*Ficus*)

Fusion — advanced technique for *Ficus*

Jerry Meislik, USA

Only one other tree that is commonly used for bonsai, the trident maple, has a similar fusing talent.

***Ficus* will also fuse with, or attempt to overgrow, rocks, and even buildings!**

Introduction

Those who have read my book *Ficus: The Exotic Bonsai*, are already aware of my passion for these trees. My appreciation for *Ficus* (figs) goes back 27 years, to when I lived in Florida and came to discover the wonder of natural banyan trees. These impressive *Ficus* trees often have dense tangles of aerial roots forming great, natural arches and caves in which children can play. I also discovered that bonsai could be developed from *Ficus*! In the ensuing years, I have become even more convinced that *Ficus* were created specifically to be used for bonsai.

The features that make *Ficus* outstanding for bonsai are their durability, reasonably small leaf size, free branching and penchant for producing aerial roots. But their other unique talent is their ability to fuse to themselves and to engulf obstacles in their way.

Fusion

Fusion is just one of the many properties that can be used to improve *Ficus,* or fig, bonsai. Fusion allows figs to be grafted easily, to create one bonsai from multiple plants, to form large branches by bringing together smaller branches, to add roots and to thicken trunks. Aerial roots can be fused back to the trunk to enlarge the trunk, as well as to create beautiful surface rootage.

In nature, figs fuse to themselves if any portion of the tree is forced against any other part. Branches touching branches, branches touching the trunk, branches against roots, roots against roots and roots against the trunk will all fuse with time.

Two factors are critical for successful fusion: the parts must stay together and must not move apart with growth; and the parts to be fused must be allowed to grow vigorously. Wire, electrical ties or plastic wrapping twine can be used to keep the pieces from moving apart. Rubber or plastic protectors must be placed around wire to prevent the bark from being scarred. The parts to be fused must grow strongly, without any trimming, as slowing down the growth in any way delays the fusing process.

Grafting

Grafting is quite simply placing parts of the tree together in such a way that the parts fuse or grow together. In a sense, grafting is just using the fig's natural, super-strong fusion instinct.

Free grafts are the most difficult since the alignment of the vascular layers must be accurate for the graft to succeed. The end of a woody donor stem is shaped into a "V" and inserted into a chiseled notch on the host plant. The graft is secured with plastic tape and enclosed in a plastic bag into which several drops of water are inserted. Until the graft takes, the bag keeps it from drying out.

There are many types of grafts, but a few of the most useful are described below.

Forming a channel for a free graft with a chisel.

The end of the free graft is shaped into "V."

The graft is inserted into the trunk, carefully matching the vascular layers.

The graft base is secured with plastic tape and enclosed in a plastic bag.

Approach-, or in-arch-, grafting uses a long surplus branch or rooted cutting inserted into a groove chiseled into the recipient tree.

The tree before any work is carried out on it.

Creating a ¼ inch- (60-mm-) deep trough with a chisel.

A view of the trough, now ready to accept the branch.

The branch is inserted into the trough and secured with two plastic ties and a staple.

An image of an inlay graft showing the donor branch growing on its own aerial root.

A graft nailed into a channel chiseled into a trunk.

The groove should be about 2 inches (51 cm) long, and just wide enough to hold the graft firmly. The sides of the graft are shaved down to the cambium layer. Secure the graft in place with wire, tape or electrical ties. This graft is very successful since the vascular layers do not have to be accurately aligned. The graft continues to keep its vascular supply from the donor, and it is only severed once the graft has taken.

Inlay-grafting involves using a branch with a supporting aerial root removed from a fig tree.

A supply of these grafts in various sizes can be potted and grown for their eventual use as graft material. An area on the host trunk is chiseled out to receive the donor branch. The branch is secured to the host with wire, or is even nailed into place. The aerial root is inserted into the host container or is grown on in its own container. After three to six months, the graft has fused with the host and the aerial root can be removed or left in place if desired.

Thread grafts are quite easy to create and involve drilling a hole through the trunk to receive a branch that is fed through the hole. The graft branch can be from another tree or from the same tree. The hole must be drilled just large enough to allow the branch to be fed through, but no larger. All of the leaves are removed from the graft to allow it to be easily fed through the hole. Leave the terminal bud of the graft branch alone. Once the graft is successful, the graft is severed at the entry point.

Grafts will be more successful if they are allowed free growth — that means no trimming, pinching, and so on. The growth of new leaves on the graft and the flattening of the graft's stem at its junction with the host indicate graft success. Do not wire, trim or manipulate any graft for one year; its attachment is quite fragile and can break free. No sealing wax, grafting paste or other chemical treatment is needed on any of the grafts.

Whether fusing or grafting, always use trees that have identical bark colors or, better still, use plants propagated from the same tree so that the bark color will match. Initially, grafts always look awkward as young branches have a bark color that does not match the trunk, but over several years, the bark on the graft matures and matches the host.

Summary

Figs are truly a remarkable genus. Fusion is one of their unique abilities, and this can be utilized to improve them, with remarkable results. Experiment with your fig trees to fuse parts that need improving, and you will not be disappointed.

Species for warmer climates or indoor cultivation

Small-leaf jade tree (*Portulacaria afra*)

Jim Smith

A *Portulacaria* with its leaves removed.

A *Portulacaria* in leaf.

A *Portulacaria*.

The following description, by Keith Cotes Palgrave, was published in 1988 by Struik Publishers, Cape Town, South Africa.

"A fleshy, softly woody shrub or small tree up to 3 to 4 meters in height, often sprawling; occurring on dry rocky hillsides and in succulent scrub. Bark: green when young, becoming red-brown to slate gray, and smooth with conspicuous leaf scars. Leaves: simple, opposite, almost circular, about 1.5 cm in diameter, or obviate, up to 2.5 x 1.7 cm, fleshy, pale gray, pale gray-blue-green to dark green; each pair of leaves at right angles to the next along the reddish stems; apex rounded with a short, abrupt point; base tapering; margin entire; petiole very short or almost absent. Flowers: small, star shaped; sepals 2; petals 5, pale pink to purplish; stamens 5 to 7. The flowers are produced in profusion, in dense sprays at the ends of short lateral branches, making the tree beautiful (October to November). Fruit: a small capsule, about 5 mm long, 3-winged, hanging down on thin, short stalks (November to January or later).

"The leaves which are edible with a pleasantly acid flavor are eaten by African women when they have insufficient natural milk for their babies. The leaves, dried and ground, are used as snuff and the plant itself provides an excellent and valuable fodder. It is widely planted as a hedge, being quick growing, evergreen and dense; it is becoming increasingly used to check soil erosion as it binds the soil very effectively. It is now so widely cultivated that it becomes difficult, at times, to determine whether it occurs naturally or has been planted."

As yet, I have not seen one bloom in Florida; this may be due to the fact that we do not allow our plants to become sufficiently dry.

Portulacaria afra, also called elephant plant or small-leaf jade tree, is a relatively new plant in bonsai, but one that almost anyone can grow because it is succulent. Since *Portulacaria* can withstand long periods without water, they are excellent plants for beginners. Advanced students of bonsai like them because they adapt to any style and develop relatively fast.

Since *Portulacaria* is native to South Africa, it will not be possible for most people to find large, old specimens to collect, but pre-bonsai are available from bonsai dealers who sell tropical plants. When looking at an untrained plant in a nursery, it may be difficult for the beginner to visualize a finished bonsai in this tangled mess of branches, but once the unneeded branches have been removed, you can always find an interesting trunk line.

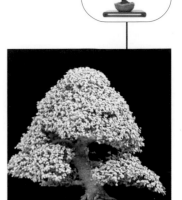

Cultivation

Portulacaria will tolerate a variety of growing conditions. Like all tropicals, it must be protected from long periods of cold temperatures below 40°F.

It can be grown outdoors in full sun or indoors if given sufficient light. The plant will develop very fast when given proper care, which includes heavy applications of fertilizer. Plants growing outdoors in full sun always need more fertilizer and water than those growing indoors.

When removing branches, all cuts should be flush rather than concave since deep cuts may leave unwanted scars. It is not necessary to seal any of the cuts.

A *Portulacaria*.

Indoors

Everyone that I have talked to who grows this plant indoors agrees that light is the limiting factor for a healthy plant. They can be successfully grown on windowsills or with artificial light. When growing it near a window, keep in mind that trees or other buildings nearby may affect the amount of light that your plant receives. If you are using florescent growing lights, it is important to place the light very close to the bonsai.

Soil

Portulacaria does not require any special soil mix. Whatever you are using for your other bonsai will probably be satisfactory. Good drainage is always important.

A formal upright *Portulacaria*.

Water

Although the plant is a succulent, it is not as particular about overwatering as most other succulents. If the soil that you are using drains well, you should not have any problems; always allow the soil to approach dryness before watering.

Fertilizer

No special fertilizer is required. Any balanced formula will be satisfactory. When repotting, I use a slow-release fertilizer that can be mixed into the soil. This can be supplemented with liquid 20–20–20 as needed. Because these plants are such fast growers, they will need to be fertilized more often than your other bonsai to maintain dark-green foliage.

A *Portulacaria* forest.

Styling

This plant adapts to any style, including cascades and forest plantings. Since it is succulent and most of the water is contained in the trunk and branches, it is not practical to style the tree with long, horizontal branches as they tend to droop because of their weight. This characteristic makes them excellent plants for full cascades. This plant tolerates drastic pruning if you allow the soil to dry completely before removing large branches and roots.

A mother-and-daughter-style *Portulacaria*.

Jim Smith in Florida.

Shohin

When creating shohin, we sometimes need to shorten a branch to a vertical set of leaves. In order to get the horizontal growth we need, it is necessary to rotate the vertical pair of leaves 90 degrees. A few turns of 1mm wire at the tip of the branch and a 90-degree twist of the last set of leaves will accomplish this.

Refinement

Refinement is achieved by removing the terminal bud from any branch that you do not wish to grow longer. Since the leaves are opposite one another, and each set of consecutive leaves rotates 90 degrees, it is possible to refine the tree by pinching and removing those buds and branches that are not growing where you wish. You can control the direction of growth by pinching back to a set of leaves that are growing in the direction that you wish the branch to grow. Pinching is the key to the refinement of any bonsai. Since *Portulacaria* is fast-growing, pinching must be performed according to a regular schedule during the growing season. Usually once a week is sufficient for large bonsai; shohin may need pinching twice a week.

Defoliation

It is usually not necessary to defoliate *Portulacaria* because of the size of their leaves. If you are growing a small shohin and wish to reduce the size of its leaves, you can use the same method as with other bonsai. The only difference is that you must allow the soil to become dry before you remove all of the leaves. After the leaves have been removed, place the plant in a semi-shaded location and do not water it until new growth begins.

Repotting

Spring is the best time to repot, but it can be done at any time if the plant is given proper aftercare. It is important that you allow the soil to become dry before repotting or severely pruning the top. Do not water until new growth appears. Keep the tree in a semi-shaded location until new growth begins, and then place it in its normal location.

Insects and diseases

I have never had a problem with insects or diseases. I learned by accident that the plant would defoliate if sprayed with a petroleum-based pesticide. If you find insects on your plant, try washing them off with water from your hose. If you need insecticide, use one that is not petroleum-based.

Propagation

This is an easy plant to reproduce. If any trimmings from your tree are left on the soil, they will root in a few weeks. Large cuttings can also be rooted. It is best to allow cuttings to dry for a day before placing them in the rooting medium. Keep them in a semi-shaded location until rooted. Large cuttings can be trimmed, shaped into a bonsai style and then rooted in a bonsai pot, using your regular bonsai soil, for an instant bonsai. Group plantings can also be created in this way.

Indoor bonsai

Tropical, exotic and indoor bonsai – an introduction

David W. Fukumoto, Kurtistown, Hawaii

Growing bonsai indoors

David Fukomoto, of Fuku-Bonsai, is from Hawaii, and is a pioneer in the growth and development of indoor bonsai. In this section, David discusses the techniques for growing bonsai indoors, and looks at one particular species in order to demonstrate his techniques. The techniques can be applied to most species suitable for growing inside.

The spirit, philosophy and culture of "True Indoor Bonsai"™

In the last fifty years, bonsai has become an international art, craft and hobby, with knowledge being shared at an explosive rate due to the unselfish leadership of that very special, mid-20th century generation.

It is necessary first to clarify terms so that you'll understand that our "True Indoor Bonsai"™ is just one tiny, highly specialized segment of the larger area that is known as "tropical bonsai," "exotic bonsai," and "indoor bonsai." Very few have heard of "exotic bonsai," which are trees of another region grown in a very different climate. Some use "tropical bonsai" and "indoor bonsai" very casually, and consider them to be the same. But they're not.

Tropical bonsai are created in the tropics by tropical-bonsai-growers who utilize the trees of the tropics. The tropics have less seasonal climatic variation, and there are ten times more tropical trees than temperate-climate trees. As bonsai becomes more popular in tropical climates, there are a huge number of plants that are being successfully trained as bonsai for the first time.

Ficus (fig) trees in Taiwan, Hong Kong, Indonesia and other tropical producing areas tend to follow Japanese bonsai style rules, and it is relatively rare to see *Ficus* bonsai trained into their natural, wide-crowned, multiple-apex, banyan shapes with aerial roots. Even in Hawaii, some hobbyists train their tropical trees into the single-apex, tier-branched shapes typical of pine trees.

Generally, tropical trees naturally grow into a shape similar to the broom style in Japanese bonsai. If you look at a picture of a zelkova elm broom-style bonsai and

A dwarf *Schefflera*.

Ficus benjamina "Peace Forest."

Tad"s "Manila Ripple" *Schefflera*.

imagine it progressively sinking into the ground, you'll be able to visualize the basic shape of mature tropical trees. Some have very short trunks and a wide, leafy crown. Others have multiple trunks. Most have "arch-type branching," and the overall profile is a rounded dome rather than a pointed triangle. In the tropics, most bonsai are grown outdoors in full sun, where growth is best and compact. In the shade, plants tend to be spindly and weak.

It would be a relatively simple matter to write about training and caring for outdoor tropical bonsai in Hawaii. But this information would not be applicable to all locations in temperate climates. In assisting customers in both cold Alaska, with its long, dark winters, and the American Southwest, where it is hot, dry and sunny, I believe that I can point out the principles involved so that each reader can make the necessary adjustments and be successful.

A dwarf _Schefflera_ mame.

Exotic bonsai

I'd like to give credit especially to Ernesta Ballard, of Pennsylvania, whom I consider to be the "mother of bonsai for indoors." During the 1950s and 1960s, Ernesta began to grow tropical bonsai and published the first book on growing bonsai for indoors. She had pretty much worked out the mechanics, but her insights and explanation of the difficulties encountered by temperate-climate growers pointed to the need to identify the lowest-light-durable houseplants in order to expand the number of people who could enjoy bonsai for indoors. And that is basically what Fuku-Bonsai did, with the help of many correspondents throughout the United States. But what is the appropriate name for this type of bonsai?

A dwarf _Schefflera_ saikei.

A _Pachira_.

The debate about "indoor bonsai"

Even back in the early days, already there was concerned, serious discussion about what these bonsai should be called. At that time, there was a shallow consensus that the most appropriate term was "bonsai for indoors." Unfortunately, the term "indoor bonsai" has become popular. Unfortunately also, there are a huge number of published stories by people who have been successful in growing a specific plant indoors for a few months. Somehow, only a few months of survival are enough to make the grower rush into print. It does not seem to matter that the plant has not produced enough new growth to train.

Junipers and pine trees can survive a few months indoors if acclimatized to low light, and there are instances where junipers have been grown indoors for more than a year. Bonsai hobbyists proudly wrote articles and produced long lists of plants that they had grown successfully for a few months in their well-lit homes, and soon the term "indoor bonsai" lost all meaning. Bonsai marketers use the term to sell tropical bonsai and imported Chinese penjing. Customers purchase them thinking that they are buying houseplants. Confusion continues.

Ficus benjamina rock aikane.

Dwarf *Schefflera*: large, high-crown banyan.

A dwarf *Schefflera*.

Ficus m. retusa "Snake Dance."

To be successful, it is important for bonsai growers to understand the needs of a specific plant and the care required in their area. No bonsai book can possibly provide specific information for all locations, and the best informational sources are probably the members of a local bonsai club.

"True Indoor Bonsai"™

When we created our export nursery in 1973, we wanted to avoid any misrepresentations or being caught up in the open ended confusion and debate over the proper terms. So "True Indoor Bonsai"™ became a Fuku-Bonsai trademarked term to include only proven, durable houseplants that can be grown in ordinary houses without supplemental light.

There are very few plants that can be used, and we've come to specialize especially in dwarf *Schefflera* (*Schefflera arboricola*). This section discusses only this plant. In order to be successful in growing bonsai in your home or office, there are three rules that must be followed.

RULE 1: Grow trees that will grow well for you in your own environment, or change your environment to meet the needs of your bonsai
Temperature: Throughout the world, with either air conditioning or interior heating, most interiors fall between 60 and 80°F (15 and 26°C), and this is the temperature range in Hawaii throughout the year. In theory, tropical plants can grow indoors, but with the proviso that you are able to provide enough light.

Light requirement: We selected low-light-tolerant plants that need only the light level available in most indoor settings. Light within 12 inches (30 cm) of a window is still inadequate to grow most tropical plants as bonsai. The fig (*Ficus*) family of plants will grow well indoors if given a much higher light intensity. Growth will improve as light levels increase, and even houseplant bonsai will grow better in bright greenhouses or outdoors in warm seasons.

RULE 2: Start with a tree that already has some character

Evaluate the trunks of unappreciated houseplants in the corner of an office, at plant-rental companies or at nurseries that specialize in interior-scaping. Starting with exciting stock will enhance your success!

RULE 3: For better growth, create optimum conditions

Homes that use air conditioning or central heating are dry, and houseplant bonsai will benefit from increased humidity. Individual trees can have humidity trays, and several can be grouped over a larger tray.

Indoor bonsai pots do not get the heat of the outdoor, direct sun, and because there is less air circulation and less evaporation, indoor bonsai take far longer to dry out than outdoor bonsai. Having the bottom layer different from the body mix creates a perched moisture layer that drains well, but also retains water vapors.

Watering and feeding: Most people overwater plants. Learn to allow plants to dry out a bit, and then water to saturation. To learn proper watering techniques, weigh the plant when it is a bit dry, sit it in a pan of water to absorb the maximum amount totally, and then weigh it again. Just by lifting the pot, you'll get to know when a plant needs watering.

Water and fertilize with "enriched water"

Create "enriched water" with just a drop or two of a very weak, liquid fertilizer in 2 pints (1.1 liters) of water. Use this to water plants using the dip-saturation method. Pour excess water back into the storage container.

Conclusion

I've been honored to work with many international bonsai masters. They have created our international bonsai era in the hope that bonsai will be a bridge to international friendship and peace. As we pass bonsai leadership to a new generation, I thank Craig for the opportunity to share my thoughts, and hope that these ideas will provide additional food for thought in your own bonsai journey!

Ficus m. retusa, an epiphyte bonsai.

A dwarf *Schefflera* "Arches."

Ficus natalensis "Benevolent Dragon."

201

John Yoshio Naka

One of the great bonsai teachers of the 20th century died in 2004. On May 19, Grand Master John Yoshio Naka died, three months short of his 90th birthday.

He was my inspiration in making the transition from bonsai artist to bonsai teacher. He was a man who was full of fun, as well as being a fountain of knowledge. His ability as a teacher, motivator, and ambassador for bonsai was unparalleled, and he is one of the people most responsible for the growth of bonsai outside Japan. John Yoshio Naka lived with his wife, Alice, and their family in California, where I visited him. Sensei Naka came to the UK for the first time in 1984, and I was one of the team of organizers for that tour. I filmed him over five weeks, and when he came to Scotland, he insisted on wearing full Highland regalia. He was also a clansman of the Japanese Naka clan, and it was great fun when he donned the outfit, complete with long johns and simmit (undershirt). I was nervous about meeting this master, but he soon put me at ease, and soon it was as though I had discovered a long-lost brother.

Universally acknowledged as the most famous and most popular bonsai teacher in the history of bonsai, John touched all of our lives. John Naka understood the meaning of humility. He never referred to himself as a "master," but always as a "student." John Naka considered the trees to be the teachers. He would easily tolerate any level of skill, while motivating you to strive for perfection.

Developed from my notes over the years, these are some of John Yoshio Naka's teachings. Some are basic, but all are important in your development as a bonsai artist.

- A bonsai should look like a tree.
- Always mark your front with a marker in the soil, such as a piece of wire.
- Start wiring from the base up, and style from the base up.
- Refine your tree from the top down.
- When working on the apex area, style that into a separate tree, and then work that apex into the overall structure afterward. Otherwise, the apex will not have definition.
- The apex should be about three times the diameter of the trunk.
- The apex, as a general guideline, should not be bigger than the dimensions of the pot.
- Increase taper by allowing the branches to grow out.
- When working on a twin-trunk tree (John called this a "catapult shape"), make the front off-center and not face-on. This will give you a more three-dimensional image.
- Do not have too many branches as that would be out of proportion to the size of the tree.
- Create jin by peeling back slivers with pliers.
- Cut out water for two or three days prior to styling or wiring deciduous trees.
- A small branch under a main branch is called an accent branch.
- Back branches are best kept longer, and front branches should be kept shorter. This is because, in an ideal bonsai shape, the tree should be leaning, or bowing, toward you. If the front branches are too long, that will entail too much "lean."
- When styling a raft, make some intermediary branches shorter as that will increase the perspective, or depth, and distance.
- When creating a cascade, cross some of the branches over the trunk to avoid having a bare trunk.
- Using a hexagonal container can be a powerful addition to a cascade style.
- Look for a stable baseline appearance for a good nebari, or surface-root structure.
- Do not repot and style at the same time.
- When removing branches from, as opposed to styling, a bonsai, you may be able to remove some roots, too.

John Naka designs a forest

John Naka was a great teacher and a great friend, and after attending so many of his workshops, demonstrations, and critiques, he still forms an indelible part of my teaching life. I try to follow his teaching by example, and so encourage younger teachers by giving them the opportunity to show what they can do. I try never to stifle them, and always to encourage new talent. Someone once said, "John is the stuff of legend." They were right.

I spent nearly two years bringing together these *Juniperus chinensis* "Blauw" trees for this demo, which was held in 1984 at the Royal Botanic Gardens Lecture Theatre, Edinburgh, Scotland.

John started sorting through the trees for the best heights and forms. He wanted to create a forest with depth. This group would be tall at the front, and would recede into the background.

The team that assisted John comprised Jim McCurrach, who took classes with John in the 1970s when he lived in America, Bill Jordan, Peter Adams and me. Peter was my teacher at the time, and Jim had been working with me as a bonsai buddy for nearly five years. Bill was one of the UK's most outstanding bonsai artists, and a RHS and Chelsea gold medalist.

John had drawn a sketch of his design on the blackboard, and we all set about wiring and shaping the trees under John's guiding hand.

The first tree is placed. This is always the most important tree in a forest composition.

The second-largest tree is next, as that determines the balance.

John determined that the second tree needed another one planting very close to it in order to start creating depth. More individual refinement was needed on the trees, and John did that himself.

Placing each tree was achieved by using peat muck to hold them in position until the roots were established.

The pot was constantly turned to make sure that the planting was vertical and that no tree was crossing at the side or front, blocking another from view. The pot was a very expensive, handmade, yamaki pot that I had imported from Japan for this special demo.

The small trees were now made and inserted into the group. It is not evident, but Jim's continual cleaning of the working was both necessary and a great boon to John as he worked on the composition.

Peter and John refine the remainder of the junipers prior to positioning. I should mention that preparing material for this demo was extremely hard work, and I had traveled all over the country to obtain suitable specimens of varying heights and trunk thicknesses. Organizers always have this problem when inviting teachers for conventions. The old adage, "You only take out what you put in" is never truer.

The last tree is placed.

The completed group is checked for crossing branches, trunks and so on. Some trunks are tied together for stability until the roots develop in the following year.

The group pictured three months later, as the foliage starts to develop. Peter Chan obtained the group shortly afterwards and it formed part of his collection at Herons Bonsai in England.

John takes a *claidheamh da laimh*, or two-handed sword, commonly known as a claymore. This is, of course, one of my regular, Scottish carving tools. (Photographed by Craig Coussins; Ian Baillie took the final shot.)

chapter 5
Asian bonsai
and penjing

Singapore penjing

Some outstanding collections exist around the world, and I have taken many wonderful images that illustrate the beauty of masterpiece bonsai and penjing. I still read in some Western books, and on some websites, that penjing do not have a bonsai form. Indeed, it is generally thought in the West that if a styling is an abstract form, as opposed to a recognized form, the tree is a penjing. The inference is that the tree is of poor quality. Of course, that annoys me, and, indeed, annoys most people who study penjing. I have seen outstanding trees as penjing from various Eastern cultures, and many of these are of a much higher standard than some of the bonsai that I have seen in places where the term "penjing" is not given respect. It is about cultural, as well as design, differences.

Singapore is an island republic between Malaysia and Indonesia, and while it is only one area of outstanding penjing development, it is by no means the only area where quality and excellence is a byword for penjing. There are superb collections of international quality around China, and there have been superb advances made in recent years by some of the many Chinese designers in the field of pentsai and penjing. I quote from the United States National Arboretum in Washington: "Today, it is very difficult for those outside the bonsai and penjing communities to tell the difference between bonsai and penjing. Both are outstanding examples of Asian art expressed in plants and natural materials, and both forms continue to evolve."

The quality of the bonsai or penjing in Singapore is exceptional, and this is a unique look at some inspirational trees. On page 139, one of Singapore's penjing masters, Lim Keow Wah, made a foray into the mountains of China to collect wild *Juniperus chinensis* from their natural home. Master Lim showed me around some of the wonderful private collections of Singapore, and while we cannot show everything in this book, I hope that this will give you a taste of what is here. A visit to the Chinese Jurong Penjing Gardens is a must when you stop over in Singapore.

The Chinese Jurong Penjing Gardens

Singapore is a very exciting place to visit on the way to other countries. I often pop in to visit my many penjing friends from the Singapore Penjing and Stone Appreciation Society, who create some exceptional trees. Year-round growing conditions help, but they are also superb artists.

The trees grown here are nearly all tropical specimens, growing at latitude 1°N in a humid climate averaging 86°F (30°C). The penjing on display in the Chinese Jurong Penjing Gardens are from China, Japan, Malaysia, Indonesia, and Thailand. In some cases, I have abbreviated the names of the species shown here, which include different *Ficus* species, *Podocarpus* ("*Pod*"), *Wrightia religiosa* ("*Wrt*"), *Pemphis acidula* ("*Pem*"), *Casuarina* ("*Cas*") and *Baeckea frutescens* ("*Baek*"), part of the Myrtaceae group. Many are over 6 feet (2 m) high, while the rest range between 1½ and 5 feet (0.5 and 1.5 m).

There were originally more trees, but the collection still numbers in excess of a thousand trees and is well maintained (a constant battle, due to the exceptional growing conditions) by the recently appointed young curator, Vincent Quek Hock Keng. A large team of gardeners keeps the trees watered, and the place is very tidy. I chose images to illustrate the high standard of the penjing.

There is a large display of rock landscape arrangements without plants, too (see page 240), and a very interesting collection of gongshi scholar's stones.

Wrightia religiosa.

Ficus retusa.

Casuarina.

Wrightia religiosa.

Wrightia religiosa.

Lake Taihu Stone and *Wrightia religiosa*.

Wrightia.

Sagaretia theezans in flower.

Wrightia.

Casuarina.

Wrightia.

Wrightia.

Podocarpus.

Podocarpus.

Podocarpus and *Wrightia*.

A garden view.

A garden view.

Wrightia religiosa.

Podocarpus — a huge-size tree, one of a pair that acts as guardians for the garden.

A view from the Ting (pavilion).

A garden view.

A beautiful view from one of the many hidden areas in the garden.

Trees grown in lucky symbols for presentation at New Year or other festivals.

Casuarina.

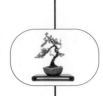

Sagaretia.

A view across the pond to the rockscape penjings.

A landscape created by the
Cheng Tai Nursery.

A lake view of the Chinese Jurong Penjing
Gardens in Singapore.

The curator of the gardens, Vincent Quek Hock
Keng, takes a short break.

The Ting, or pavilion.

Throughout the gardens, there
are places to sit and admire.

Vincent stands with a *Wrightia
religiosa* penjing.

Wrightia religiosa are often
grown into good-luck shapes for
special occasions.

Penjing — Tay Kock Wah, Singapore

Tay Kock Wah has been designing exceptional shansui-penjing landscape scenes. Here are two of his beautiful and elegant interpretations.

Singapore Penjing and Stone Appreciation Society exhibit

Some of the varied and interesting pentsai individual trees (or shumu penjing) that have been created by members of this popular club. The images have been supplied by Lim Keow Wah.

Cong Ben, *Wrightia religiosa*.

Kah Hui, *Wrightia*.

Kah Hui, *Wrightia* on rock.

Bing Xing, a medium size *Pemphis acidula*.

Bing Xing, a small *Pemphis acidula* pentsai.

Cao Hua, *Baeckea frutescens*.

Cao Hua, *Caesapinna ferra*.

Cao Hua, *Pemphis acidula*.

Chin Kiat, *Ixora* "Sunkist."

Enghui, black pine.

Eric, juniper.

Gui Feng, *Premna*.

Hanping, Itogawa juniper.

Jah Kim Chuan, a *Wrightia religiosa* pentsai.

Jiang Shui, *Vitex quinata*.

Kah Hui, cascade *Wrightia*.

Xiang, *Wrightia*.

Yen, *Wrightia*.

Yian Xiang, *Ixora* "Sunkist."

Yong Qiang, *Wrightia*.

Yu Qian, *Ehretia microphylla*.

Yue Chuan, *Wrightia religiosa*.

Yue Hua, *Premna*.

Yue Jiaop, *Baeckea*.

Premna.

Quek H K, *Pinus thunbergii*.

Robert Ko, *Juniperus chinensis*.

Sheng, *Wrightia*.

Yue Po, shi hang lian.

Yue Hua, Ficus.

Yue Hua Lim, *Pemphis*.

Yue Hua, *Pemphis*.

Zhang Fu, *Wrightia*.

Zhang Fu, *Wrightia*.

Zheng Ta, *Casuarina equisetifolia*.

Zheng Ta, *Triphasia trifolia*.

Zhi Hua, *Wrightia*.

Miniature trees

The Singapore Penjing and Stone Appreciation Society (SPSAS) exhibit, by Ng Chin Kiat and Lim Choon Gik. These are some images from one of the exhibitions held each year in Singapore. In the other photographs, the mini-penjing specialist Ng Chin Kiat takes us around his own collection. Mr. Ng is a member of the SPSAS. Lim Choon Gik looks after the collection of the Bonsai Club of Yuhua Community Club. Mr. Lim shows us some of the smaller trees in this large collection.

Cao Hua, group.

Chin Kiat, group.

Chin Kiat, group.

Gui Feng, group.

Hanping, group.

Nicholas Choo, group.

Rong Hui, group.

Zhun Yu, group.

Binsing, *Pemphis* **group.**

Wrightia religiosa.

A *Wrightia religiosa* **being held by Lim Choon Gik.**

**A Bonsai Club of Yuhua
Community Club (BCYCC) tree.**

**A creation of the Bonsai Club of
Yuhua Community Club.**

A BCYCC tree.

Another creation of the BCYCC.

A multibranched BCYCC tree.

A tiny BCYCC tree.

Pots of wonderful miniatures.

The pots sit on sand; the roots grow into the sand to develop trunks.

A Singapore Penjing and Stone Appreciation Society tree.

Pots sitting on sand.

At the Bonsai Club of Yuhua Community Club in Singapore.

More pots sitting on sand.

Pots with roots growing outside them that are cut off regularly.

A *Wrightia religiosa* being grown in the form of a good-luck symbol.

A magnificent SPSAS tree.

More SPSAS creations.

Ng Chin Kiat, of the SPSAS.

The Bonsai Club of Yuhua Community Club

The Bonsai Club of Yuhua Community Club is another Singapore club. Some clubs associate with each other and can exhibit together or share facilities. However, they tend to have their own, specialized area for their members' trees as many live in apartments and do not have facilities to keep penjing. To facilitate the community spirit of each part of Singapore, areas of land are set aside for community clubs covering a number of general interests, and some of these extend to large display areas without much, if any, security. That brings up the obvious question for Western bonsai collectors who have had trees stolen. The answer is that there are still some countries where you can not only feel safe, but where that kind of petty crime is either nonexistent or irrelevant. Lim Choon Gik took me around this collection.

The Bonsai Club of Yuhua Community Club is a penjing club.

Lim Choon Gik.

A *Ficus*.

***Wrightia religiosa*.**

***Wrightia*.**

Another *Wrightia*.

***Wrightia*.**

Pots sitting on sand.

***Juniperus chinensis*.**

Camellia.

***Ficus retusa*.**

Singapore nursery collection — The Cheng Tai Nursery

The Cheng Tai Nursery has some of the largest trees in pots that I have seen. I have been known for working on, and creating, very large bonsai, but some of these would be a little too large for me. They are all carefully manicured, and are used in landscape plantings, as well as in penjing arrangements. The nursery has been very generous in supplying trees for the Chinese Jurong Penjing Gardens exterior display.

Craig with a *Casuarina equisetifolia* (Casuarinaceae).

A *Wrightia religiosa* measuring 6¹/₂ x 8 feet (2 x 2.5 cm) at the Cheng Tai Nursery.

Lim Keow Wah with a *Wrightia religiosa*.

Lim Keow Wah alongside another large *Wrightia religiosa*.

A large *Casuarina* at the Cheng Tai Nursery in Singapore.

A *Wrightia religiosa*.

chapter 6
bonsai and
penjing display

Displaying bonsai both in exhibition and in your collection at home is in itself an art.

Display of bonsai

One of Japan's leading bonsai masters, Kunio Kobayashi, has been awarded the Sakufuten Award in Japan several times for his magnificent bonsai art, some of which is shown here. Mr Kobayashi also shows us some of his excellent trees in tokonoma settings throughout this chapter.

White Pine.

Black Pine – "Old Crane". Crane is believed to live to 1000 years.

Black Pine.

Wisteria Sinensis.

Satsuki Azalea.

Satsuki Azalea - Kikako.

Japanese yew (*Taxus cuspidata*), winner of the Prime Minister's Award, Kunio Kobayashi.

How to display bonsai

Introduction by Craig Coussins

It is important to learn about placement in the display of a bonsai. When displaying your bonsai or penjing, natural light is the most important of the elements, as light and shade affect its growth. Climatic conditions determine the health and vigor of the tree but, above all, the correct placement of a completed bonsai will enhance the grower's surroundings.

This satsuki azalea (*Rhododendron indicum*) has a special name, and that is "Kikaku" ("Tortoise and Crane"), meaning something that lives very long. (Kunio Kobayashi.)

The special name of this black pine (*Pinus thunbergii*) is "Rokaku," or "Old Crane" (the crane was believed to live for a thousand years). Kunio Kobayashi won the Kokufu-ten Award with this.

A *Wisteria* created by Kunio Kobayashi.

Satsuki, "Kikako." (Kunio Kobayashi.)

Exhibiting bonsai is always a popular part of this hobby, and the best way to illustrate what does, and does not, work is through pictures.

The tokonoma

Tokonoma literally means "alcove room." There are various theories about the origin of the alcove. It may originally have been a sleeping alcove, built just large enough for bedding. The alcove floor was then raised above the level of the floor. Over the years, the alcove was enlarged to the size of two mats, and was then contracted again to one raised mat. The alcove thus became the honored seat for a guest of high rank. The other mat was placed at floor level. On occasion, a cozy alcove was formed by surrounding it with screens.

From the Kamakura period (1185–1333) to the latter part of the Muromachi period (1392–1568), the alcove had a raised floor and could be used as a seat or a platform. By the end of the Kamakura period, a Buddhist picture had been hung on the wall and became the focal point of the tokonoma. A board on which to display objects, *oshiita,* was set before the wall-hanging. On it were exhibited a vase of flowers, an incense-burner, and a candlestick. These three objects are important to Buddhism, and are referred to as the three implements, *mitsugusoku*. In the Muromachi period, it became customary to omit the candlestick and to hang up a scroll with a Zen priest's calligraphic inscription.

By the Momoyama period (1568–1615), the alcove took on its familiar form and was used principally for displaying treasured art objects. The size and arrangement of the alcove varied according to the diversified tastes of the tea masters. An old record, for instance, mentions an alcove 70 inches (180 cm) long attached to a tea-ceremony room used by Murata Jukou (1423–1502). This alcove was pasted with white Japanese paper called *torinoko,* and had frames that were covered with black lacquer. Takeno Jouou (1502–55) preferred a smaller alcove and tea-ceremony room. Sen Rikyuu (1522–91) used alcoves with styles that are familiar today. Characteristics from both the *shoin*-style alcoves and the alcoves found in tea architecture were fused to produce the alcove common to ordinary dwellings

Tokonoma are called by a great variety of names, such as *kamizadoko* ("upper seat alcove") and *shimozadoko* ("lower seat alcove"). Sometimes, tokonoma are named for the particular width of the alcove, such as *daimedoko hondoko*, plain wooden alcove, *itadoko*, a *tatami*-mat alcove, *tatamidoko* and many more.

A single falling leaf in the wind and rain clearly describes fall with this Scot's pine.

Considering the placement in a tokonoma
Paul Goff

The basic intention when displaying bonsai should be to hold the viewer's attention while conveying an overall feeling of harmony. If more than one object is included in the display, i.e., a bonsai, table, accent plantings, figurines, stones, or hanging scroll, it is appropriate that the items bear relevance to one another, and that the artist uses them in a minimal way to convey an understanding of a particular time, place, or season in the natural landscape.

Whether the arrangement is on exhibition benching or in a specially designated display alcove (tokonoma), the artist must employ a measure of sensitivity in terms of spacing, size, and proportion between the elements to ensure that a well-balanced, harmonious living picture is achieved that delivers a positive message to the viewer.

The placement of such an arrangement must be carefully considered. At an exhibition, individual spaces are often defined by lengths of bundled bamboo on a bench at a convenient viewing height for standing spectators. A plain background is essential, and the designated space must then be perceived as a frame for the intended picture.

The use of tokonoma allows the artist to organize his or her display without distraction in a specially constructed alcove or niche. Neutral or earth colors are normally combined with natural timber in its construction. A small tokonoma of less than 3 feet (1 m) in width may be elevated to a convenient viewing height, while a larger space, up to 10 feet (31 m) in width, is often set lower for seated contemplation.

This mountain pine changes little throughout the year, but by employing a neutral scroll, the mood and season can be implied by thoughtful use of illustrations.

The Western preoccupation with clutter must be avoided at all costs when making an artistic arrangement. A simpler, minimal statement, using three or fewer objects, is preferred. In fact, some will argue that, if any one of the objects is removed and the story remains the same, that object was not essential in the first instance. In other words, bonsai with accent-planting, bonsai with scroll or bonsai with suiseki, or any combination of two to three of the aforementioned components, may be sufficient. The restricted number of elements will, it is hoped, stimulate the spectator at an intellectual level to unravel the relevance of the objects in terms of their association, in order to reveal the artist's intended picture.

To aid the artist in getting his or her message across, it would be wise to study some established guidelines. To be bound by hard-and-fast rules would be foolish, and may result in the restriction of uplifting artistic playfulness.

Look, listen, and learn from successful displays and arrangements and, of course, observe our greatest teacher, nature itself. When placed in a restricted setting, a bonsai with any added accessories will set up a degree of correspondence between those items. Here, relevance is paramount. If an appropriate association does not exist, a unified composition of beauty and harmony will not emerge. The opportunity for an exhilarating moment is then lost. It is not difficult, but it must be thought out and planned well. As with other tasks associated with the creation of bonsai, preparation proves invaluable.

Proportion and spacing between the items in the display deserves important consideration in order to retain a harmonious unity of oneness, yet creating the illusion of great depth and spaciousness. No one piece should dominate the arrangement, and the visual movements of the individual pieces should ultimately focus the viewer's attention to the center of a scalene triangle linking the visual centers of the bonsai, scroll, and accent components. These points of the triangle may also be seen as representing heaven at the top, man at the mid-point and the earth at the base.

An icy, cold moon on the hanging scroll confirms a winter setting for this English oak.

At the end of winter, melt waters come rushing down from the mountains — a perfect accompaniment for this mountain pine.

So what observations and guidelines should we consider? If you decide to follow Japanese traditional bonsai display, it will become necessary to understand the categories of *shin*, *gyÛ*, and *sÛu*, which mean "formal," "semi-formal," and "informal." Each category can be broken down into further subdivisions of shin, gyÛ, and sÛu, resulting in a very specific arrangement; for example, shin gyÛ (a formal bonsai set in a semi-formal way). The tree, being the key subject in the display, determines the style, i.e., formal, semi-formal, or informal. Special occasions, times of celebration or the reception of an important guest may be acknowledged by setting a formal or shin display in the tokonoma. A formal-upright pine, juniper or yew in a rectangular pot with vertical sides is considered appropriate here, and traditional elements that are also suitable for the occasion may be included as accent, accessory, or scroll.

A semi-formal, or gyÛ, display would feature an informal bonsai as its centerpiece. This may be a deciduous or flowering tree in a pot with softer, curved lines. The gyÛ display is ideal for identifying the season.

The informality of the sÛu display allows the more free-form approach, and may include literati or cascade bonsai styles. Here, it is appropriate to express the season or simply the mood and atmosphere.

Basic considerations for setting out an individual display at an exhibition or in a tokonoma will usually begin with a bonsai as the centerpiece, although this is not always the case, as suiseki or kusamono can often be prime subjects. The artist must decide if the display should convey a special occasion or the mood of the location at a particular time of day or season. When considering the season, ideally, a subtle hint of nature's progression toward the coming season should be included. With the combination of no more than three objects, plus the power of suggestion, it should be possible to influence the spectator in his or her understanding of your intent. It is crucial that, as the exhibitor, you avoid any degree of repetition in terms of materials, finishes, and colors in the content of your arrangement. For example, to include dwarf flowering alpines as accent in a glazed pot in association with a flowering bonsai also in a glazed pot

This simple arrangement of snow-covered mountains and a snowdrop tells of a cold day toward the end of winter.

Courting doves on the hanging scroll enhance the joys of spring with a flowering-cherry group bonsai.

A scalene triangle should link the visual centers of the scroll, bonsai, and accent. Here, a common hawthorn is accompanied by an accent of feverfew and a single butterfly on the scroll — the perfect summer day.

Lakeside summer — a Chinese juniper leans over the water's edge, while rush grass with blackberry occupy the boggy shore. Being set on a bamboo raft stand accentuates a waterside theme. On the scroll, a single boatman is spotted in the mist on the lake.

A winter clump of English elm stands before a snow-covered peak, while snowdrops indicate warmer days ahead. Here, we can clearly see how depth is created in the display by placing the accent slightly forward of the key object.

Fall lakeside with a European larch — the scroll implies a setting in the hills, shortly after a rainstorm. The accent is miniature geranium.

On the scroll, an owl flies past a golden moon; it may be nesting in the hollow of the field maple. Here, the accent comprises a continuation of fallen leaves from the bonsai and the emergence of fall fungi on the piece of old tree stump.

The rising-sun theme on a scroll and a stork as the accessory would make ideal companions to a formal-upright, evergreen bonsai in a New Year display.

would be considered inappropriate on two counts: the repetition of glazed containers and the presence of flowers in two instances.

Similarly, a rock planting as the main subject would not sit well alongside a suiseki as accent, or even a scroll painting that includes a mountain landscape, because of repeating themes. Links between component parts of the display must be made by subtle implication, and may often involve intellectual interpretation by the spectator to reveal the picture. Returning to the rock-planted bonsai, the accent could be alpine grass with a container that is totally unlike that of the centerpiece to imply the location of trees and rocks at altitude, or even a figurine of a bird or animal found in this environment. The scroll could be used to indicate the season by incorporating a flower, grass, an insect, the sun or moon, clouds, or mist, but, in any event, must not illustrate any other element repeated in the arrangement.

The sun and moon are excellent indicators of time and season. The Japanese often use the rising-sun theme for new life or a new beginning in a formal New Year display. The sun seen behind the clouds, or through the mist, may help with time of day, but avoid using a setting sun as this may imply the end of a period or death. A deep orange or blood-red full moon (harvest moon, as we know it) may suggest late summer/fall.

It is natural to expect that endless variety and numerous combinations of display elements are possible. Therefore, the outline here is simplistic, but, I hope, will inspire the enthusiast to look further into the world of traditional bonsai display.

Beyond the tokonoma

Craig Coussins

The room around the alcove is a space for mediation, entertaining special visitors or showing your prized bonsai, scroll or suiseki.

Tsukeshoin (shoin)

From 12th to the 19th century, Japan was divided into autonomous territories under the control of feudal lords, or daimyo. The samurai, or warrior class, protected daimyo families against their enemies. During the Momoyama period, the daimyo developed the tsukeshoin, a big room used to receive large numbers of visitors. Formal rules of behavior meant that the receiving of visitors became an artform in itself. The shoin is characterized by a set of formal features, collectively known as zashikikazari. These include a shallow decorative alcove (oshiita), staggered shelves (chigaidana), a built-in table (tsukeshoin) and an ornamental doorway (choudaigamae).

Hondoko

The hondoko is a formal alcove (tokonoma) in this large room. It may be positioned to one side of a plain wall with staggered shelves (chigaidana) and a built-in, short cupboard with sliding doors beside it, or it may be placed directly in the center of such a wall. In either case, the alcove pillar (tokobashira) is square, with chamfered corners. The floor is made of thick, straw mats (tatami), and the wall is papered. A simpler hondoko may have plain, brown, clay walls. Both the framing boards and the alcove pillar are often coated with black lacquer, creating what is called the shin, or true formal style. Some hondoko have lacquer frames with a polished cedar log used for the alcove post. Still others may have a frame with corners cut by an adze (chouna) and/or post(s), or even a log frame with bamboo shoots chamfered on the bottom parts (takenokomentori). This style is referred to as semi-formal (gyou). The floor is raised, framed and covered with tatami mats.

Belgian tokonoma, _Acer_ by Gilbert van Est.

Newby tokonoma, juniper "Blauws" by Craig Coussins.

Goyo-Matsu white pine by Kunio Kobayashi.

Black pine (*Pinus thunbergii*), the winner of the Prime Minister's Award at Sakufu 10, by Kunio Kobayashi.

Kunio Kobayashi

Mr. Kobayashi has been a much-appreciated, headlining demonstrator at many conventions and special events around the world. He has been the recipient of many major awards in Japan, and he recently set up a new bonsai school in Japan that caters to bonsai students from other countries. Mr. Kobayashi is a very experienced bonsai artist who has created a magnificent collection housed in his nursery. His trees have won many prizes. In 1983, he took the first prize at Sakufuten, the Japanese professional bonsai exhibition. In 1999, he was awarded the Prime Minister's Award for an unprecedented third time, a record that, extraordinarily, he broke again in 2000. I have included some of his outstanding work throughout the book, and especially in this tokonama section, where some of his wonderful bonsai are exhibited in the tokonama, or alcove, setting.

Tsukebashira

A post placed at the exterior corner of the alcove, which projects (tsukeshoin) onto the veranda in an aristocratic-style dwelling. This post is 20 to 30 percent smaller in scale than the main posts. It is not a supporting post, but usually has something attached to it, for example, a shelf with a groove.

Chigaidana

Staggered shelves are considered part of the shoin-style decoration. Together with the decorative alcove (tokonoma) and attached desk (oshiita), the *chigaidana* became established at the end of the Muromachi period (late 16th century) in the formal reception room (*zashiki*). They are usually located at the side of the decorative alcove.

Katoumado

A *katoumado* is mainly associated with Zen-style, *zenshuuyou* temple buildings. The window has an ogee-type, pointed top, with a series of "S"-like curves on either side of the peak.

盆栽

chapter 7
rocks and miniature landscapes

Here we look at other forms of art that are often exhibited with bonsai and penjing — rockscapes, with and without plants. In some major collections of bonsai and penjing, there are outstanding collections of rockscapes, placed on trays to illustrate the natural landscapes, mountains, and features of the local environment.

A Utah penjing landscape

Craig Coussins

Here, I create a distant Utah landscape image. Perspective planting, using tall and small trees, creates the illusion of distance. The rock was collected in North Wales by Alan Dorling and Kevin Bailey. It is hard limestone, similar to the Lake Taihu stone from China, and was a gift from my friend, Kevin Bailey. The rock has two natural water pools and an interesting "hoodoo" formation on the right side that resembles formations in Bryce Canyon and Hurricane Sands Desert, Utah. Indeed, I was inspired by a particular rock formation.

We first mix a peat muck using 50/50 modeling clay and peat-based potting compost.

The mix is placed in two areas — one on the extreme right side and another higher up, on the left side.

The trees to be styled are cuttings from *Cryptomeria japonica* "Nana."

We style the three trees that we are going to use.

The first tree is placed so that it gives structure to the design. The second tree gives lateral body to the design, and the final tree gives depth. This last tree may not be strictly necessary in this particular composition, but we will live with it for a while.

The soil is carefully added to each tree, and peat muck is used to locate and hold the trees in place.

Short-grain moss gives a grasslike effect.

Slightly longer-grain, darker moss is used in the "distant" tree to give added depth.

The final composition is called "Hoodoo Canyon."

Choosing the trees for the Utah penjing landscape.

The *Cryptomeria* cuttings were five years old.

Styling the trees.

A small tree before styling.

The same tree after styling.

This will sit at the back.

This will have a jin.

Creating the jin.

The completed jin.

Before styling.

After styling.

Limestone river rock from Wales. This is like Chinese Lake Taihu stone.

We made a clay-and-peat mix.

We made a wall for the soil.

We put the soil into the new "pot."

We pressed fine moss into the clay–peat wall.

The first tree is placed.

The second tree provides lateral dimension.

Placing the trees so that they work together.

Placing the back tree to provide depth.

Pressing in moss and holding it with bent wire.

Utah penjing landscape, by Craig Coussins.

Creating a penjing perspective landscape

I created these landscapes when I was in Australia, using local rocks and available material. I also ran a workshop in Brisbane, at Tess Simpson's Bonsai Northside nursery, where some very talented artists spent the day with me. Everyone went away with some stunning landscape images.

I drew some ideas for a penjing perspective landscape.

The rocks came from a local nursery.

I explained to the others the different designs that I could make with the raw material.

I used *Juniperus procumbans* for the trees.

This was not difficult material to work with, and comes out well in this kind of design.

This tree was less than 5 inches (13 cm) in height.

It turned out nicely. In all, I used five trees of different sizes.

I placed the rocks, using peat mixed with clay to secure them.

Building the "mountain" to create depth.

The tray was now ready to receive the plants.

The main tree will be at the front; the smallest tree will be at the back.

The next tree is placed on the mountain base.

The trees are almost set now.

Ric Roberts is assisting me in planting the moss and accent plant and adding sand.

The final image — the front.

The final image — the back.

At the Brisbane workshop for penjing landscapes.

The Nullarbor Desert inspired me. (Nullarbor is a corruption of Latin and means "no trees.")

A penjing landscape created at the Brisbane workshop.

An Australian rockscape that was made at the Brisbane workshop.

A mixed-species landscape made at the workshop in Brisbane.

A penjing landscape created at the Brisbane workshop.

A penjing landscape viewed from the end of the pot in Brisbane.

The front. This is an unusual, and an effective, design.

Rock plantings

These images show examples of landscape planting. Each country's bonsai artists have their own ideas of how to illustrate their native landscape. Here we have landscapes created in South Africa, Scotland and Australia.

Vietnam rock landscape planting. (DB.)

L Pieters, *Cotoneaster microphyllus.* (ABA, DW.)

K. Le Roux, landscape with rocks. (ABA DW.)

K. Le Roux, low mountain landscape.

K. Le Roux, African rockscape. (ABA DW.)

Craig Coussins, pines on rock (grafted seedlings).

Craig Coussins, pines on canyon.

Rockscapes in nature

When I travel, I enjoy searching out some of the world's many astonishing landscapes. This section is designed to inspire designers of landscape plantings and displays of rocks with and without plants.

Glasshouse Mountains, Brisbane, Australia.

Arches National Park, Utah, at dawn.

Cathedral Gorge, Nevada. A moonscape made of amazing, soft limestone.

A rockscape in Devon, England.

The Pinnacles, Australia.

Fairy Glen, which is situated deep in the north of Wales.

Land's End cliffscape, England.

A natural stonescape on Pike's Peak, Colorado.

An evening rockscape in Monument Valley.

Monument Valley: an archetypal rockscape.

El Torcal, near Malaga, Spain, is an amazing mountain, full of unbelievable stone landscapes. I often visit this area when I go to Spain.

Sulfur terraces, Yellowstone, Wyoming. These pools have been created by mineral deposits that constantly bubble up through the soil. I have seen similar terraces in different parts of the world, and am always fascinated by the wonderful shapes that are created.

Looking into the hoodoos of Bryce Canyon, in Utah.

Basalt crystals in Fingal's Cave, Staffa, in Scotland.

Zion Canyon, Utah. This stunning canyon is easy to visit from Las Vegas. Leave your car in the Zion Park visitor center and take the shuttle bus into the canyon, after which you can explore on foot.

Sulfur pools, Yellowstone, Wyoming.

Northeastern Utah's Flaming Gorge. To get the best light on the colors of the rocks, I took this shot from the top of one of the mountains just after dawn. Now, this is a landscape that I really would like to recreate.

El Torcal, Spain.

Stone formations on Skye, Scotland.

The Cuilins of Skye. This extinct volcanic crater is a very beautiful sight when viewed from across the bay.

A hidden lake glimpsed in the northeastern Wyoming Mountains.

Arches National Park, Utah, is known for its "arches." This landscape is very inspiring to the landscape creator.

Pinnacles Desert, Western Australia. I spent the afternoon, evening and the following dawn trying to get the best image. These rock formations are limestone pillars, which are covered and exposed by shifting sands every five thousand or so years. Truly a place to visit!

Red Plateau, Hurricane Sands, St. George, Utah. This rock feature is difficult to reach, but is the one that inspired me to make my Hoodoo Canyon (see page 230).

The Twelve Apostles, Great Ocean Road, Victoria, Australia. One recently fell down, so now there are only eleven "apostles." I spent some time taking shots because the weather was unsettled. There were still eleven when I left.

Pike's Peak, Colorado, is 14,100 feet (4,300 m) high. I was fascinated by the high desert rockscapes once I had passed the tree line at around 10,000 feet (3,000 m). Katharine Lee Bates wrote the words to the classic American anthem "America the Beautiful" after her trip to the summit in 1893. Pike's Peak is an isolated peak on the front range of the Rocky Mountains, located in central Colorado. It forms a massive backdrop to Colorado Springs as one travels west off the eastern plains. This shot looks down over one of the smaller peaks, which has these unusual rocks scattered over the top.

Emma Matilda Lake in Grand Teton National Park, Wyoming, at dawn. I have photographed this lovely rockscape at different times of the day, but this is my favorite shot. The trees by the lake are very old, and I had this landscape in mind when I made the Pine Canyon landscape.

Balanced rocks in the Garden of the Gods, Arches National Park, Utah. I think that this picture can speak for itself. I was lucky both to see the sight in this light and to capture it on film.

Balanced rock in a thunderstorm at sunset in Arches National Park, Utah.

Jasper striations in seaside cliffs, Devon, England.

Singapore exhibition of penjing landscapes
A blend of stone and plants

Guo Hua, island landscape.

Guo Hua, *Baeckea virgata*.

Guo Hua, *Baeckea virgata*.

Guo Hua, yin-shi landscape.

Hai Zhou, landscape.

Stone arrangements, Chinese Jurong Penjing Gardens, Singapore

These images show how Chinese artists have interpreted their landscapes. These are pure rockscapes, inspired by nature, without any plants. However, they could be planted or temporarily arranged with plants.

chapter 8
associated arts

International Arts and Garden Center, Singapore

This is one of the large nurseries in Singapore that specialize in penjing, and its collection is very large. It also has a section selling a selection of gongshi and entrance-hall, large-size Lake Taihu scholars' stones.

The International Arts and Garden Center.

Lake Taihu stones.

Lingbi gongshi.

Lingbi gongshi for sale.

Large Lake Taihu stones for sale.

Smaller stones.

Gongshi, or scholars' stones.

A line of giant gongshi ready for sale.

I call this "The Running Man." Now, that's a good gongshi for a sports shop.

Suiseki, shanshi and gongshi

The Scholars' Home — He She Chuang collection.

Buffalo — Singapore Penjing Gardens.

Gongshi — Coussins collection.

Mountain Stone — Coussins collection.

Hugely popular with bonsai growers, suiseki and gongshi (Chinese scholars' rocks) are miniature landscapes that, in many cases, can assist growers in the design of their bonsai. We look at what a suiseki is and how it is used and displayed (shanshi is Chinese suiseki).

Suiseki and shanshi

Suiseki are small, naturally formed stones that are admired for their beauty and their power to suggest a scene from nature or an object closely associated with nature. Among the most popular types of suiseki (pronounced "suu-ee-seck-ee") are those that suggest a distant mountain, a waterfall, an island, a thatched hut or an animal. "Shanshi" is the Chinese form of "suiseki."

In the 6th century, emissaries from the Asian mainland brought several such stones to Japan. The Japanese adapted the art to suit Japanese tastes, and have practiced it to this day.

The term "suiseki" means "water stone." It is derived from the ancient custom of displaying miniature landscape stones in trays filled with water, and from the association between suiseki and classical Oriental landscape paintings of mountains and lakes.

Within the last decade, an increasing number of non-Japanese, particularly Western bonsai and tray-landscape enthusiasts, have discovered the special beauty of suiseki.

Gongshi

Traditional scholars' stones are known as "gongshi". The collection of gongshi dates back nearly two thousand years. Many gongshi consist of very hard limestone and are strangely shaped. They can help in meditation and in mind-focusing. Feng shui is an essential part of a Chinese home and, given the rapid growth in the free market, many young Chinese business people have been buying these works of nature's art for their modern-design homes.

Dragon Stones — England and Wales, Coussins collection.

The Chinese characteristics of a good stone are:
1. *Xiu* (pronounced "shyow") — lovely, shapely form and overall image;
2. *Lou* (pronounced "low") — flowing or cascading;
3. *Tou* (pronounced "toe") — piercing, translucency, allowing air and light through;
4. *Qi* (pronounced "chee") — amazing, astonishing, breathtaking movement;
5. *Zhuang* (pronounced "jew-ong") — powerful, massive, solid, foundation.

I asked Kemin Hu to explain some of the stone types. Kemin Hu is America's leading authority on gongshi. Some scholars have praised her as being the most renowned woman connoisseur of Chinese scholars' stones in the past four hundred years.

Kemin Hu is the author of two books: *The Spirit of Gongshi: Chinese scholars' Rocks* and *scholars' Rocks in Ancient China — Suyuan Stone Catalogue*. Both books have successfully helped to spread the appreciation of scholars' stones to the West.

Contemplation Stone — Wax Stone, Singapore Penjing Gardens.

Kemin's passionate interest in scholars' stones comes from her father, Hu Zhao-Kang, who was a noted connoisseur of Chinese bonsai, penjing, gongshi and Chinese antiquities for fifty years of his life. Kemin's own vast collection of scholars' rocks has been featured in numerous exhibitions, including a one-hundred-piece exhibit in the Chinese scholars' Garden, Staten Island Botanical Garden, New York, in 2002.

Gongshi is a stone that helps with meditation by reminding the viewer of a place, object or animal. In the Tang Dynasty (618–907), scholar–officials and other sophisticated people started to collect these stones. Representing landscape or animals, these stones were very big, and were generally placed in the garden so that the owner could feel at one with nature. Small stones, which were preferred for viewing inside the house, derived from the enjoyment of seeing the bigger stones in the garden.

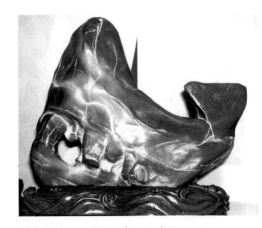

Fish Stone — J.Tan Chengtai Nursery.

Gongshi were also presented as tribute objects or gifts to leaders of communities or neighboring countries. When the stones reached Japan and Korea in the later Sung Dynasty, in around 1160, they were an instant hit.

Listed below are some of the types of stones, and the illustrations show their variety.

Lingbi stones

Ranked first among the four types of famous Chinese scholars' rocks, lingbi stones are found in the Lingbi county of Anhui province, China. They are formed from fine-grained, delicately textured limestone, and lie deep in the red mud of the Qingshi Mountains. Naturally shaped, they need no cutting or carving. Depleted after generations of mining, high-quality lingbi are now quite rare. They are hard, and an ordinary knife cannot cut them. Their mineral composition is such that they produce a metallic, resonant sound when tapped. Hence they are also called "resonant rocks" (bayinshi). Lingbi were sometimes used for making chimes, and are thus also known as "chime rocks." Lingbi rocks are beautiful and clear-cut, with a frame of soft lines.

Taihu stones

Found mostly in the vast drainage areas of Tai Lake, limestone Taihu rocks are hard but brittle. There are slight variations between those taken from lake beds and those extracted from the land, and also between those of different regional districts. Those formed under water are more precious because of their fresh, soft color and their multiple, linked perforations, produced by years of wave and water erosion. Taihu rocks are usually large, with a pale-gray or ivory tint, and are regarded as the best garden rocks. Artificial hills made of Taihu rocks give the appearance of strange peaks looming up, or of chains of hills connected by streams and bridges, with successive peaks along narrow, twisted paths. Small Taihu rocks of good quality are rare and are meant for indoor appreciation. The beauty of Taihu rocks lies in their thinness and their wrinkled appearance, as well as in the perforations and hollows that enhance their open appearance.

Taihu Stone Gongshi — 15 x 7 x 3 inches (42 x 18 x 10 cm). He She Chuang collection.

Suiseki Baby, Craig Coussins.

Display of Lingbi Stone Gongshi — 27 x 28 x 10 inches (68 x 71 x 25 cm). He She Chuang collection.

Hut Stones — Coussins collection.

Turquoise Gongshi — 10 x 6 x 4 inches (25 x 16 x 9 cm). He She Chuang collection.

Ying stones

Traditionally produced in Yingde, Guangdong province and Guanxi province, Ying rocks are limestone with calcite deposits. Less hard than lingbi, they are often full of furrows, with twisted lines on intricately textured surfaces. Notable for their diverse shapes, they appear to embody a thousand hills and valleys, and so are well suited to representing a distant landscape. They can also represent animal shapes. The ying stone's typical thin, wrinkled appearance often shows traces of sawing and cutting, and they have distinguishable front and reverse sides. The best-known example is called "Winking Cloud Peak" in Hangzhou's West Lake, China.

Red River Stone, China — Craig Coussins.

Zibowen stones

"Wen" rocks are found in Zibo and Shandong provinces. They are decayed rocks composed of lime, granite or clay stone. Aesthetically, wen rocks have an antique simplicity. They have a weathered look, with dots or crossing lines on the surface and a variety of wrinkled forms. Among this type are aragonite rocks, which are usually black and very hard. Wen rocks portray a feeling of "pu."

Multiple Doha — Coussins collection.

Red-river stones

Red-river stones are composed primarily of quartz, and are found in the riverbed of the Red Water River in Guanxi province. There has been a growing demand for them among Southeast Asian collectors in recent years, so good examples can only be found about 65 feet (20 m) below the surface. As a result of their scarcity, there are few opportunities to see them in the West. They will, however, surely attract more attention in the future.

Craig Coussins' Suiseki and Gongshi Display.

Qixia stones

Sometimes known as xixia stones, qixia stones are from the Qixia Mountain, Qixia county, Henan province. These stones remind the viewer of caves and mountains, and are enjoyed for their beauty. Some qixia stones are very abstract and almost supernatural in form. Some look like monsters, elephants or some kind of beast suckling its young or eating its prey. The stone is a gray limestone, and the larger specimens are usually displayed on carved stands.

Camel Stone, Eel River California, 10 inches (25 cm) long — Coussins collection.

Some other stones

In addition to the ten basic gongshi types, there are laoshan green stones ("laoshan lushi"), malachite ("kongqushi"), turquoise ("lusongshi"), duan stones ("duanshi"), soapstone ("shoushanshi"), chrysanthemum stone ("juhuashi"), marble ("dalishi"), and suan stones.

Kika Seki, 9 inches (23 cm) tall — Coussins collection.

K. W. Lim's stones

My friend, Master Lim, from Singapore, not only has some wonderful penjing and incredible antique pots, but also a very nice collection of gongshi — Chinese scholars' stones. Some are obvious in their shape, and others not so clear. That is really what a viewing stone is all about: you can see what you want. This quality makes it an ideal aid to meditation.

**K. W. Lim's shanshi animal
(jasper).**

A lingbi stone.

Another lingbi stone.

A face lingbi stone.

Making stands for suiseki — daizas —

Sean Smith

Sean Smith is one of the world's leading daiza-carvers. Here, he explains a little about the background of suiseki and then shows us how to create a stand for a beautiful stone. Sean is the proprietor of Custom Oriental Wood Craft in Marysville, Pennsylvania. He has presented demonstrations, lectures, and displays throughout America and Europe, and is one of the principal organizers of the International Stone Appreciation Symposium held each year in America. Sean has made most of the daizas for my own collection.

How to make daizas

Sean Smith

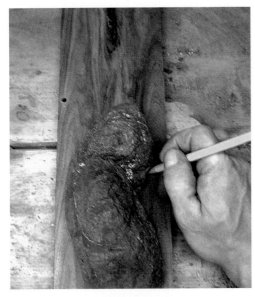

"Daiza" is the word that we use to describe the wooden, hand-carved bases that our beautiful stones are displayed on. This is one way to make your own daiza and has been my preferred way for over six years.

The next step is choosing the wood. I find hardwoods, such as walnut, mahogany and rosewood, excellent, and will use the color of the stone to determine the color of the wood for the daiza.

First place the stone on the wood. Use a sharp, number 2 pencil to trace around the outside of the stone, being very careful of the pencil's angle and width. The angle is very important as you do not want it to be too vertical or too low as that will affect the way that the stone sits in the daiza. You should not have any gaps between the stone and the daiza.

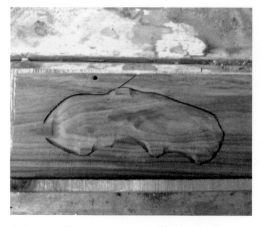

I need to work out how deep the hollowed-out shape needs to be in order to hold the stone securely. Closely following the traced line, and using a concave chisel or router, I remove the wood on the inside of the outlined drawing. Using a Dremel tool or similar, with a ⅛ inch (3.2 mm) straight-bit router attachment, I remove the remaining wood all of the way until I touch the inner edge of the drawn line.

Using a palm sander, I sand off the pencil marks and then try the stone in the new shape. The stone rarely fits the first time that it is tried. Placing the stone once more on the new shape, I again trace around the stone. This will leave a few "points" that require me to take out a little more wood. I sand off all of the pencil marks and start again. I continue to do this until I am satisfied with the fit. After getting the fit right, half of the battle is over.

The next stage is working out what style of daiza will suit the stone. A famous bonsai and suiseki teacher, Yuji Yoshimura, once said that the base was simply a part of the overall appearance of the stone. I, too, want the daiza to be handsome, but not overwhelming. The daiza is there to hold the stone, and should therefore be relatively simple, elegant and should accent the stone without detracting from it.

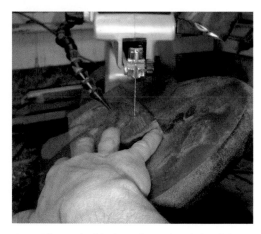

Once I have decided on the style of the daiza, I draw an outline of the number of walls. I place the stone carefully back into the wood. This helps me to determine the width of the wall. Using the outer edge of the stone as a guide, I trace the line, following the contours of the stone. I use a router to cut along the edge of the outer side of the new line. This creates the first wall of the daiza.

The next step is to cut out the daiza with a scroll saw. I do this by using the wall as a guide. I keep both pieces of wood. I then place the newly cut-out daiza on the stone (never the other way around as that could easily damage the wooden surface of the daiza). I now need to draw an outline of the feet.

Once the stone is fitted tightly into the daiza, I mark the position and shape of the feet in the sides of the walls with my pencil. Setting my router according to the height of the feet, I place the daiza upside down back into the wood stock. I place the daiza back on the stone and check that the feet are correctly positioned and are balanced.

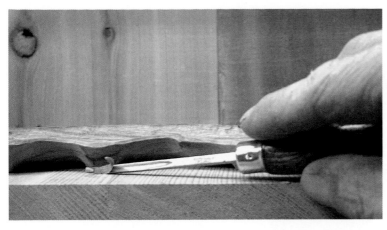

I now shape the daiza, using sharp carving chisels. Once the rough shaping has been completed, I start the sanding process, starting with 120 grit and working down to 400 grit. The final sanding is done with 0000 steel wool.

Now I apply a lacquer finish, which seals the wood.

Once dry, the daiza is ready to accept the stone, be displayed and then be admired for a lifetime.

Mountain stone collected by Felix Rivera, in the Eel River, California. Daiza in walnut made by Sean Smith (Coussins collection).

Index

Ancient Juniper in Great Basin National Park.

azalea, satsuki   78–82

bonsai, *see also* penjing
   African   92
   American   93–95
   Australian 96–103
   Belgian   110–12
   displaying 220–28
   English   113
   Japanese 104–6
   definition of 13
   heights   89
   indoor   22, 23–25, 194, 195,
            197–201
   outdoor   22, 26–27
   Spanish   107–8
   Swiss   109
   viewing   45–46
buds
   cutting   57
   plucking 57–58, 81, 182

carving 117–22, 132–35
climates 18–19, 78, 194
cuttings 79

daiza   249–51
dead wood   170–72
   creating   173–77
diseases 37, 53

eastern white cedar (*Thuja occidentalis*)
  169

feeding 33–36, 53, 66, 182, 195
fig (*Ficus*)   183, 190–93
foliage 66

fungicides   37, 38

gongshi, *see* scholars' stones
grafting 191–93
groups   123–24, 148–49
   forest   69–71, 203–4
   on rock   72–74

insecticides   37, 38

landscapes, miniature   230–31, 232–34
larch (*Larix*)   166–68
light 26–27, 58, 182
lighting 24–25
lime sulphur   38

maintenance   75, 81–82, 84
maple (*Acer*)   181–82, 184–89
misting 18
moss   39

Naka, John Yoshio   202–4

penjing, Singapore   206–18
pests   37–39, 53, 181
pine (*Pinus*)   51–59, 62–65, 114
potting 32, 80, 83, 164, 195
problem-solving 76, 80, 144–45
pruning 40, 56, 80, 182

ramification   66, 182
refinement   66
repotting, *see* potting
rocks   72–74, 235, 239, 240–41
   in nature   236–38

sandblasting   174–77

scholars' stones 243, 244–47, 248
shanshi, *see* suiseki
slabs   49
small-leaf jade tree (*Portulacaria afra*)
   194–96
soil   28–31, 58, 80, 195
   Akadama   29
   Kanuma   30
   Kiryu   30
   pH levels   31
styles   80, 86–92
   Pierneef image   148–49
   windswept   48, 49, 50
styling   50, 54–55, 62–65, 67, 68, 69,
   69–71, 76–77, 125–27, 128–31,
   136–38, 139–41, 142–43, 144–45,
   146–47, 150, 152–53, 154–57,
   158–60, 161–63, 164, 165, 166–68,
   178–80, 195
suiseki   244

terminology   86–88, 89
tokonoma   220–28
tools   40, 60–61
trees in nature   20–21, 65, 149, 151,
   170–72
trunks
   fusing   183, 184–89, 190
   twin 165

uro   151

watering   14–18, 52, 66, 80, 181,
   195

wiring   41–44, 80

Portulacaria Forest.

Credits

Thanks to:

1. Kevin Bailey, who acted as my personal technical editor for this book. www.actionvideo.freeserve.co.uk/vocbsindex.htm
2. Fuku-Bonsai Cultural Center & Hawaii State Bonsai Repository, PO Box 6000 (17–856 Olaa Road), Kurtistown, Hawaii 96760. Tel: (808) 982-9883; e-mail: sales@fukubonsai.com; URL: www.fukubonsai.com
3. Tony Tickle. www.yamadori.co.uk
4. Paul Goff, for his generosity and kindness in creating the tokonoma images for his section. www.paulgoff.co.uk
5. Sean Smith. bonsai-suiseki.com
6. Frank Mihalic. www.wildwoodgardens.com/wildwood/index.html; e-mail: sales@bonsaionlinemagazine.com
7. Sally McGeoch Botanic Gardens Trust (Sydney).
8. Jaime Plaza, Wollemi pines images, Botanic Gardens Trust (Sydney).
9. Sue Stubbs, Wollemi pine bonsai, Botanic Gardens Trust (Sydney).
10. Jerry Meislik, Whitefish, Montana, USA. www.bonsaihunk.8m.com
11. Doug Phillips, California — a great mate and whisky-appreciating buddy. www.dugzbonsai.com
12. Chase and Solita Rosade. www.rosadebonsai.com
13. Harry Harrington. Bonsai4me.com; e-mail: Harry@links4bonsai.com
14. Guy Guidry. www.bonsainorthshore.com
15. François Jeker, France.
16. Jim Smith, whose kindness has inspired so many in Florida and elsewhere. www.jimsmithbonsai.com
17. Trevor Smith, who helps me to make some lovely bonsai.
18. Nate Clifford, from Colorado.
19. Rob Atkinson, England. robert@atkinson6473.freeserve.co.uk
20. Lim Keow Wah, Singapore, whose help was instrumental in the Singapore presentations. www.geocities.com/lkwahsg/entryPage.htm
21. Chai Kwei Foon, Ng Chin Kiat, Chin Choon Poon, Hoo Hai Chew, Tay Kock Wah, International Arts & Cultural Gardens Pte Ltd, Cheng Tai Nursery Pte Ltd, and members of the Singapore Penjing and Stone Appreciation Society.
22. Lim Choon Gik, from Bonsai Club of Yuhua Community Club, Singapore.
23. Vincent Quek Hock Keng, curator of the Jurong Gardens bonsai exhibit, Singapore, who opened up the gardens on the Monday closing day to allow me full access to photograph the collection, while keeping me cool with ice-cold grass jelly.
24. Jasline Tan and Kim Kwang Tan, Cheng Tai Nursery Pte Ltd, Singapore.
25. Georg Reinhard, Switzerland, whose kndness is sincerely appreciated. www.swiss-bonsai.ch
26. John Armitage, England. JArmitageBonsai@aol.com
27. Jean-Paul Polmans, Belgium.
28. Danny Use and Ingrid Van Lomel, Gingko Nursery, Belgium, a couple that I truly admire and respect as friends and bonsai enthusiasts. www.ginkgobonsai.be
29. Erwin Verheyan and Frank de Decker, along with the members of the Mechelin Bonsai Club, for supporting me on my visits to Belgium and keeping me well-lubricated with Trappist beers.
30. Serge Clemence, Switzerland — Mountain Pine Demo-ABBA.
31. Dan Barton. www.dan-barton.co.uk, ABBA.
32. Organic Pest Control. www.extremelygreen.com
33. Rod and Shellie Smith. *The Art of Home Gardening,* by Rod Smith. Rod Smith, 8946 NW Dick Road, Hillsboro, OR 97124. rod.shellie@verizon.net
34. Yoshiro Nakamizu, Bonsai Network Japan. www.j-bonsai.com
35. Peter Warren, apprenticed at Mr Kobayashi's nursery in Japan, for his generosity of spirit in understanding the difficulties of a writer researching material for a book.

36. Chris Cochrane, for teaching me what is, and what is not, rocket science.
37. Reiner Goebel, Canada. www.rgbonsai.com
38. Kunio Kobayashi, Japan. www.kunio-kobayashi.com
39. Insect research: Drees, Bastiaan M, and Jackman, John A., *A Field Guide to Common Texas Insects*, Gulf Publishing Company, Houston, Texas, 1988.
40. He Shi Chuang, scholars' stones. www.szsssf.com/body.htm
41. Kemin Hu, America's leading authority on Chinese stones. www.spirit-stones.com
42. Mariusz Komsta and Daria Podgorska for their help with Japanese material.
43. Masahiko Kimura, for allowing photography by Mariusz Komsta to be used in this book.
44. Australia: many people who helped me and became firm "mates," including Megumi, Alex and Brian Bennett of Imperial Bonsai Nursery in Sydney, Shane Bryce, Richard Roberts, Paul Lee, Arthur Robinson, Jan Briggs, Paul Sweeny, John Oldland, Dianne Boekhout, Frank Hocking, Richard Poli, Michael Clarke, Elaine and Alan Bradshaw, Tess Simpson, Ray Nesci, Kingston Wang, N. Udaya, Leong and Sue Kwong, Peter Odin, Derrick and Sue Oakley, John Di Vincenzo, Chris di Nola, Don DeLuca and Michael Edger and the staff of the Sydney Chinese Gardens.
45. Ric Roberts of Sydney, whose generosity of time and material allowed me to achieve so much for this book.
46. New Zealand: Robert Langholme and Simon Misdale, my close friends.
47. The committee of the New Zealand Bonsai Association, Lindsay Muirhead and the many friends in NZ who worked with me and allowed me to take images of their bonsai.
48. The Japanese Architecture and Art User's System. www.aisf.or.jp/~jaanus. JAANUS is the online dictionary of Japanese architectural and art historical terminology compiled by Dr Mary Neighbour Parent.
49. Todd B. Hanson, USA.
50. George Le Bolt, New Jersey
51. Jim and Linda Brandt, Pennsylvania.
52. The board and members of the Mid-Atlantic Bonsai Societies (MABS), who allowed me to take images of the MABS Convention exhibition.
53. The board and members of the Association of British Bonsai Artists (ABBA), for allowing me to use images taken at various ABBA events.
54. Irv and Rhoda Kleiman, New York, who have been so very kind to me on my visits.
55. Ken Moore. gadgets4bonsai@yahoo.co.uk

I have probably overlooked some names, and sincerely apologize for that oversight. Please let me know if I have excluded your input into this book, and I will make a huge apology on my website at www.bonsaiinformation.com.

Craig Coussins